My Family at Work

My Dad Works on a Farm

By Sarah Hughes

Children's Press
A Division of Scholastic Inc.
New York / Toronto / London / Auckland / Sydney
Mexico City / New Delhi / Hong Kong
Danbury, Connecticut

Photo Credits: Cover and all photos by Maura Boruchow
Contributing Editors: Jeri Cipriano, Jennifer Silate
Book Design: Michael DeLisio

Visit Children's Press on the Internet at:
http://publishing.grolier.com

Library of Congress Cataloging-in-Publication Data

Hughes, Sarah, 1964–
    My dad works on a farm / by Sarah Hughes.
      p. cm. – (My family at work)
    Includes bibliographical references.
    ISBN 0-516-23178-2 (lib. bdg.) – ISBN 0-516-29574-8 (pbk.)
    1. Dairy farming—Juvenile literature. 2. Dairy farmers—Juvenile literature. [1. Dairy
      farming. 2. Occupations.] I. Title.

SF239.5 .H84 2000
636.2′142—dc21

                                                                                    00-047534

Contents

My name is Miguel.

This is my dad.

My dad works on
a **dairy** farm.

He raises cows.

Our cows wear tags.

The tags are like
name tags.

They help us tell one
cow from another.

9

It is time for the cows to eat.

We lead them inside.

11

Our cows eat **grain**.

It is time to milk the cows.

Dad uses a **machine** to milk the cows.

15

We get a lot of milk
from our cows.

17

The milk fills a big **tank**.

A truck will take the milk to the milk **plant** to be bottled.

19

Our work is done.

Now it is time for a snack.

BE
HEALTHY
DRINK
MILK

21

New Words

dairy (**dair**-ee) of or about milk

grain (**grayn**) the seed of corn, oats, wheat, or rice

machine (muh-**sheen**) a device that does work

plant (**plant**) a building in which something is made

tank (**tangk**) a large container for liquid

To Find Out More

Books
Hooray for Dairy Farming!
by Bobbie Kalman
Crabtree Publishing

Milk: From Cow to Carton
by Aliki
HarperCollins

Web Sites
Adams Family Farm
http://www.Adamsfamilyfarm.com
See pictures and read about a real family farm in Vermont.

Moo Milk: A Dynamic Adventure into the Dairy Industry
http://www.moomilk.com
This site has games, quizzes, and information about how milk is made.

Index

About the Author
Sarah Hughes is from New York City and taught school for twelve years. She is now writing and editing children's books. In her free time she enjoys running and riding her bike.

Reading Consultants
Kris Flynn, Coordinator, Small School District Literacy, The San Diego County Office of Education

Shelly Forys, Certified Reading Recovery Specialist, W.J. Zahnow Elementary School, Waterloo, IL

Sue McAdams, Certified Reading Recovery Specialist and Literary Consultant, Dallas, TX

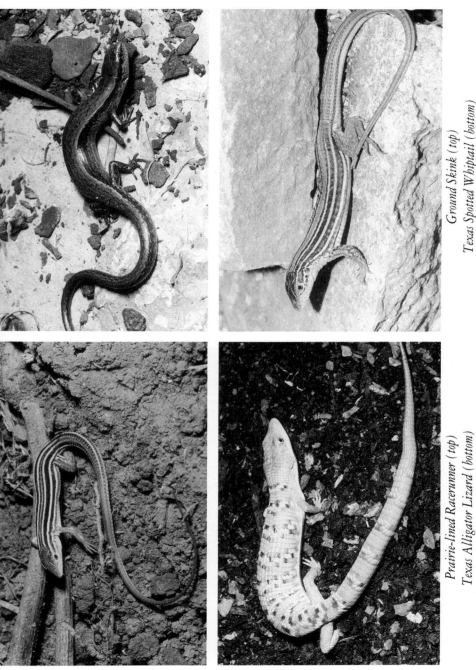

Ground Skink (top)
Texas Spotted Whiptail (bottom)

Prairie-lined Racerunner (top)
Texas Alligator Lizard (bottom)

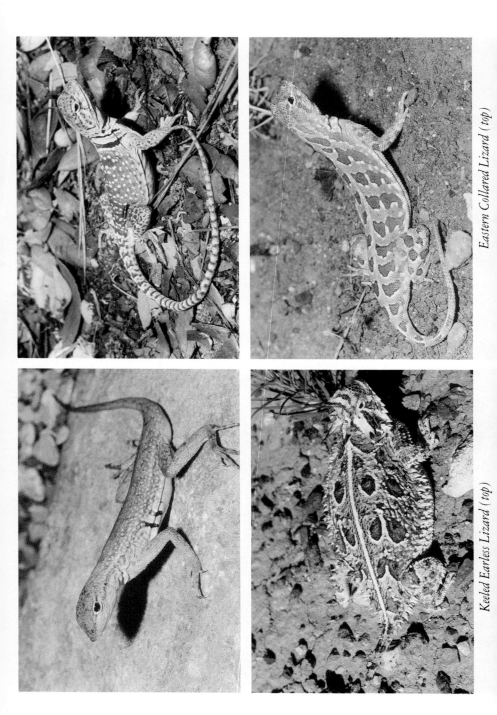

Keeled Earless Lizard (top)

Eastern Collared Lizard (top)

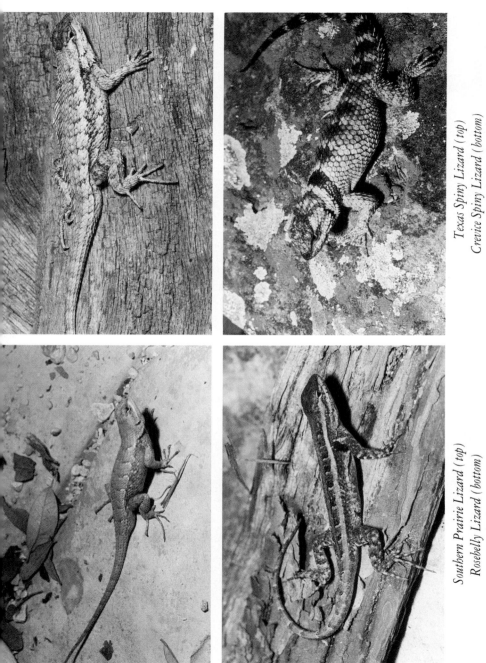

Texas Spiny Lizard (top)
Crevice Spiny Lizard (bottom)

Southern Prairie Lizard (top)
Rosebelly Lizard (bottom)

Three-toed Box Turtle (top)

Texas Tortoise (top)

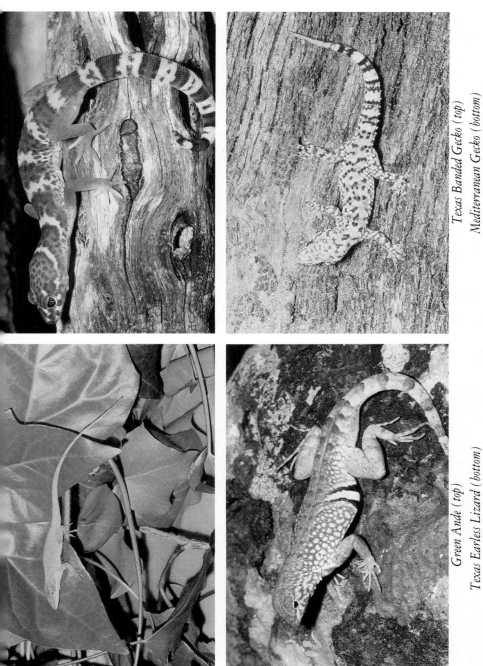

Texas Banded Gecko (top)
Mediterranean Gecko (bottom)

Green Anole (top)
Texas Earless Lizard (bottom)

Western Slender Glass Lizard (top)

Yellow Mud Turtle (top)

Common Musk Turtle (top)
Cagle's Map Turtle (bottom)

Texas River Cooter (top)
Red-eared Slider (bottom)

Southern Prairie Skink (top)

Eastern Tree Lizard (top)

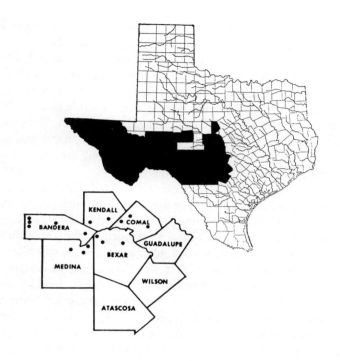

CREVICE SPINY LIZARD

Sceloporus poinsettii poinsettii Baird and Girard 1852

This spiny lizard is a large, flat-bodied, rock-dwelling member of the genus *Sceloporus*. Its distribution in South Central Texas is limited to the Edwards Plateau and the Balcones Escarpment, cutting across Medina, Bexar, and Comal counties. The range continues west from the Edwards Plateau through the Trans-Pecos region into southern New Mexico and south through the states of Chihuahua, Coahuila, and Durango in Mexico.

Identification: A broad, light-bordered, black neck collar (about 2½ to 3 or more scale lengths wide) makes an excellent field identification mark. Juveniles exhibit dark dorsal markings that appear as crossbands extending down on the sides, alternating with smaller light bands. These distinct markings continue from the back of the head to the tip of the tail. The juvenile's head appears mottled and lighter in color than the

51

dorsal markings, with a round spot between the eyes and a light cross-band across, just in front of the eyes. Adult dorsal coloration ranges from gray, greenish-gray, black, to white. Crevice spiny females tend to retain the black, gray, and white juvenile characteristics. The ventral surface of the female is usually white, although frequently a faint blue area can be seen on the throat and ventral surface. In males the pattern usually fades with age, with the exception of the neck and tail markings, and may have a bright blue color on the throat and underside. The blue-colored ventral patches on the male are bordered with black on the inner edges.

The large dorsal scales are keeled and pointed. They number from 31 to 41 from the head to above the vent. Other identifying characters include large supraoculars in 2 rows, and 9 to 18 femoral pores.

Similar species in South Central Texas include the Texas spiny lizard (*Sceloporus olivaceus*), which does not have a dark neck collar, even though the lizards are of comparable size. The southern prairie lizard (*Sceloporus undulatus consobrinus*) and the northern fence lizard (*Sceloporus undulatus hyacinthinus*) are distinguished from the crevice spiny lizard by their smaller size, smaller dorsal scales, and the absence of a dark collar across the neck. *S. u. hyacinthinus* also has a relatively complete dark line running along the rear area of the thigh. The much smaller rosebelly lizard (*Sceloporus variabilis marmoratus*) possesses large, pink ventral patches and has smaller dorsal scales. The collared lizard (*Crotaphytus collaris*) has a larger head, double collar, and granular non-spiny scales.

Size: The average adult size ranges from approximately 8½ to 12¼ inches (21.6 to 31.2 cm) from the snout to the tip of the tail. Unlike *Sceloporus olivaceus,* the males of *Sceloporus poinsettii* are slightly larger than the females (Fitch, 1978).

Behavior: These elusive diurnal lizards are wary of approaching humans. If approached, they will usually move to the opposite side of the large rock or boulder upon which they are sunning or run into a rock crevice to escape. Such crevices provide excellent protection from potential predators, such that even if a potential predator grasps one in a crevice, the lizard inflates and wedges itself even more tightly in place, making it very difficult to pull it out. These lizards are most easily observed on sunny mornings, as compared to other times and conditions. They may be reluctant to abandon their rocky position when approached or may return to approximately the same spot within a few minutes after the intruder has left. This behavior is usually modified during the afternoon, when the lizard's basking temperature is higher, and it may seek refuge directly into a crevice.

Food: The diet of this saxicolous (rock-dwelling) species includes many arthropods, but it is considered primarily an insectivore. Food recorded in the diet includes grasshoppers and crickets, weevils, wood-boring beetles and darkling beetles, cockroaches, mantids, termites, flies, true bugs, large ants, caterpillars and moths, and terrestrial spiders. Also included occasionally as food are flowers, berries, soft buds, and leaves.

Habitat: The habitat is primarily restricted to rocky canyons, rim-rocks, bluffs, cliffs, hillsides, and to other rocky outcrops of the Edwards Plateau in South Central Texas, but also includes rock walls and stone buildings in areas of infrequent human use. This lizard uses crevices along rock-walled canyons, rocky outcroppings, or boulders to escape predators as well as the extreme heat of the day.

Breeding: *S. poinsettii* is a viviparous lizard, producing a single litter of approximately 7 to 12 young each year. Mating occurs in the early fall, with live birth following in late May, June, or early July. Gestation thus usually extends over a period of several months, a pattern that differs from the multiple clutches of most oviparous *Sceloporus* species. Newborn lizards range from 2½ to 3 inches (64 to 76 mm) in total length, with young from large litters of significantly smaller size than those from small litters. Sexual maturity is attained during the second mating season after birth, at approximately 16 or 17 months (Ballinger, 1973).

General information: Known and possible predators of the crevice spiny lizard include birds (e.g., roadrunners), certain lizard-eating snakes, skunks, opossums, ringtails, and domestic cats.

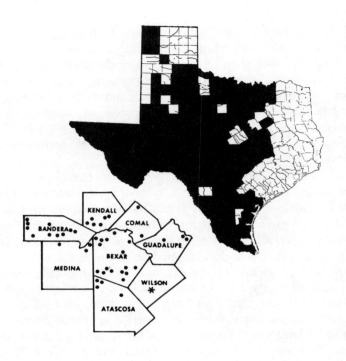

SOUTHERN PRAIRIE LIZARD

Sceloporus undulatus consobrinus Baird and Girard 1854

This widespread subspecies of *S. undulatus* inhabits most of South Central Texas and ranges from southwestern Oklahoma to extreme southeastern Arizona, southward into Mexico. It is especially common in the rocky hillside terrain of South Central Texas. This diurnal lizard is a habitat generalist, unlike the other area *Sceloporus*. The species as a whole, which occurs over most of the central and eastern U.S., differs from most iguanids in that females are larger than males; the size ratios of the sexes, however, vary geographically (Fitch, 1985).

Identification: A relatively light, distinct to faint, longitudinal dorsal stripe extends from the side of the head along either side of the back, down onto the base of the tail. These white or light yellow stripes may not be conspicuous on some individuls. On females, dark dorsal crossbars or

54

spots may border the light stripes. The dark dorsal spots or crossbars are reduced on males and are usually placed between the dorsolateral light stripes. The ground color is a light to reddish brown. *The male usually has two small, dark (sometimes darker-bordered) blue patches widely separated (or sometimes fused) on the posterior underside of the throat,* and two large, light blue, elongated patches along each side of the ventral surface. Females usually have a uniform white color on the ventral surface.

The relatively small dorsal scales number 35 to 47 from the back of the head to above the rump. Femoral pores range from 11 to 21, with over 70 percent of individuals having 16 or more (Smith, 1946).

The distribution of the northern fence lizard (*Sceloporus undulatus hyacinthinus*) borders the range of the southern fence lizard along the Gonzales-Guadalupe and Wilson county lines, with substantial intergradation of the two extending north and south through these counties and along the eastern section of the South Central Texas area. The northern fence lizard is distinguished from the southern fence lizard in having vertebral dorsal markings that are expanded as an undulating series of broken or wavy bands across a brown ground color, and by possessing a fine dark line between the eyes. Moreover, males usually have dark, dorsal tail bars. An additional distinguishing feature is that 80 percent of the northern fence lizards have 15 or fewer femoral pores, whereas the southern prairie lizards have 16 or more, 70 percent of the time (Smith, 1946). All these differences are rather vague, and some difficulty can be expected when attempting to allocate individuals from within or near the intergradation zone to either subspecies.

Other similar lizards in the region include the Texas spiny lizard (*Sceloporus olivaceus*), distinguished by heavily keeled, pointed dorsal scales, and the crevice spiny lizard (*Sceloporus poinsettii poinsettii*), which has large scales and a dark collar band across the neck. A superficial similar species, the rosebelly lizard (*Sceloporus variabilis marmoratus*), also has small scales and is of comparable size. It is unique, however, in that it has paired, pink ventral patches and a superficial skin pocket behind the thigh.

Size: The average adult size ranges from approximately 4½ to 7 inches (11.4 to 17.8 cm) from the snout to the tip of the tail. As is true with several other *S. undulatus* subspecies, females tend to be slightly larger than males.

Behavior: This lizard has a well-defined home range (Mather, 1976) and usually selects a sleeping site in close proximity to its evening basking location. Apparently, environmental factors and potential concealment are criteria that affect the selection of a sleeping site, which may be used nightly thereafter. Activity periods include midday activity in late fall, winter, and early spring, and midmorning and late afternoon activity during the late spring and summer.

The southern prairie lizard tends to be slightly more arboreal than the rosebelly lizard (*Sceloporus variabilis marmoratus*) and generally uses higher perching sites (Mather, 1976). It may become more terrestrial during late fall and early spring. According to Mather (1976), thermoregulation in this lizard is similar to other *Sceloporus* species. He documented an average cloacal temperature of approximately 94 F. (34.03 C.) for active lizards on sunny days, and reported decreased cloacal temperatures on days with cloud cover.

Food: The diet includes a wide variety of terrestrial insects. Food preferences include grasshoppers, crickets, beetles, true bugs, caterpillars, centipedes, and spiders. Additionally, Garrett and Barker (1987) reported snails as food items.

Habitat: This subspecies is generally found in a variety of areas, from open prairies and plains to mountains. It is recorded from the mountains in West Texas up to 6,500 feet above sea level. In West Texas these lizards are found in canyons which contain springs that support trees like pinon or juniper. In South Central Texas, however, they are found in association with mesquite brushlands, mesquite scattered with juniper along ravines with grasses, mixed woods, gravelly hills, wooded floodplains, river bottoms, trees in open areas, postoak-blackjack, and open sandy or rocky terrain. They are commonly seen perching on logs, bases of plants or trees, and rocks, and take refuge in small mammal burrows or in trees to avoid predation.

Breeding: Sexual maturity in this lizard is reached during the first summer of growth although they do not reproduce until the following spring (Tinkle and Ballinger, 1972). Mating takes place in late March and continues through mid-July. Limited data suggest that most females lay their 7 to 9 eggs per clutch in April, May, and June or July, and, depending on reproductive condition and age, they may produce 1 or 2 clutches per year. In South Central Texas hatching occurs from mid-June through mid-August. Hatchlings usually measure from 1³/₄ to 2 inches (45 to 51 mm) in total length.

General information: Predators of this species are numerous and undoubtedly responsible for a majority of the broken and regenerated tails found on almost one-fourth of the lizards. Comparatively little is known, however, about the details of life history for this lizard.

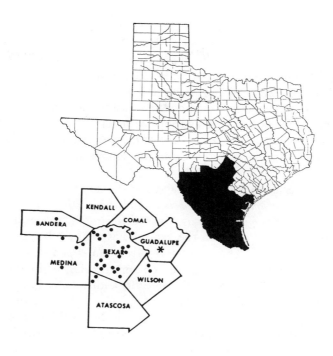

ROSEBELLY LIZARD

Sceloporus variabilis marmoratus Hallowell 1852

The rosebelly lizard is a subtropical species found in Hays, Comal, Bexar, and Bandera counties, south through the thorn brush savanna habitats of the Rio Grande plain, and thence southward into Mexico and Central America.

Identification: Identification characters include *pale dorsolateral stripes which extend from the corner of each eye to the tail, with a row of brownish blotches down each side of the middorsal line.* The top of the head is occasionally a copperish-brown, with the sides of the head a striped pale yellowish cream. The ground color for female lizards is generally olive-brown, with males usually a lighter brown in color. *Males are distinctly marked on each side of the belly by a large, pinkish-colored area* margined by blue, changing to black. This dark blue color extends along the otherwise light ventral surface, upward onto the dorsal body to form a *dark*

57

spot in the armpit area. There are smaller ventral markings along the margin on the groin in front of the hind legs. The ear area may be margined with orange, and some individuals may have dark markings on their legs. A unique characteristic for identification of this species is the *small pocket of skin at the rear base of each thigh.*

The relatively small, keeled dorsal scales number from 54 to 72 (usually more than 60) and average approximately 63 or 64 scales from the back of the head to the base of the tail. Ventral scales number approximately 56 for this subspecies, and the femoral pores vary from 10 to 14.

Similar species in South Central Texas include the southern prairie lizard (*Sceloporus undulatus consobrinus*) and the northern fence lizard (*Sceloporus undulatus hyacinthinus*), both differing in the absence of large, pinkish-colored areas on the ventrals, as well as the absence of the thigh skin pocket. The Texas spiny lizard (*Sceloporus olivaceus*) is larger and has heavily keeled and pointed dorsal scales, while the crevice spiny lizard (*Sceloporus poinsettii poinsettii*) additionally has a light-bordered, black neck collar marking.

Size: The average adult size for this relatively small lizard is about $3^3/4$ to $5^1/2$ inches (9.5 to 14.0 cm) in length. Male lizards average siightly larger than females (Fitch, 1978).

Behavior: This primarily terrestrial, diurnal lizard is active during midday in late fall, occasionally during the winter and in early spring. During late spring and summer, this activity pattern is shifted to mid-morning and late afternoon. The rosebelly lizard occasionally forages through a covering of leaf litter in association with trees, giving it a somewhat camouflaged appearance when hunting insects. Females have a considerably smaller home range than do males. The average summer cloacal temperature of active rosebelly lizards is approximately 94 F. (34.5 C.). These cloacal temperatures tend to decrease with cloudy conditions. The author has seen them in South Central Texas on warm days during the winter, occasionally basking at the base of mesquite trees or in residential woodpiles in the suburbs of San Antonio. They have also been documented climbing on prickly pear cactus, shrubs, fence posts, and basking on the trunk of a small oak tree. During late fall, winter, and early spring they become extensively terrestrial (Mather, 1976), rather than arboreal.

Food: The diet includes insects such as beetles, crickets, grasshoppers, and other insects. Arachnids, such as spiders, are also taken.

Habitat: The habitat includes mesquite, bushes, fence posts, prickly pear cactus, and occasionally around rocks. A large population in San Antonio inhabits the Cibolo Creek bottom, where they are found living on and around trees along masses of vines and weeds on steep banks. They are also found south and east of San Antonio, commonly among mesquite, living around the base of trees and in piles of dead and cut mesquite timber. Other locations include near Hondo, in heavily timbered creek bottomland, and south of Somerset, in flatlands covered with mixed timber. The northernmost limit of the range in South Central Texas extends partially into the Hill Country near Medina and Helotes. This species is occasionally found on rocks along the base of limestone bluffs around Leon Springs and Shavano Park in Bexar County.

Breeding: Males and females of *Sceloporus variabilis marmoratus* become sexually mature by their first spring (Mather, 1976). Mating may take place in Texas in late March and in June (Fitch, 1985), and South Central Texas females produce 2 clutches of approximately 4 or 5 eggs per clutch. These eggs are often deposited in the soft soil and dry humus at the base of small trees, or under decaying matter or rotting logs. Eggs, which measure $5/8$ inch (16 mm) by $1/4$ inch (7 mm), are deposited in late March and June, with hatchlings appearing in June through August. Hatchlings usually measure $1\frac{1}{2}$ inches (38 mm) in total length at birth.

General information: A rosebelly lizard from Uvalde County regenerated not only its tail but actually regenerated a long, strange-looking, tail-like, curved limb with no digits or claws (Mather, 1978). This interesting occurrence was the first record of natural limb regeneration in a North American species of lizard. The type locality for *Sceloporus variabilis marmoratus* is San Antonio, in Bexar County.

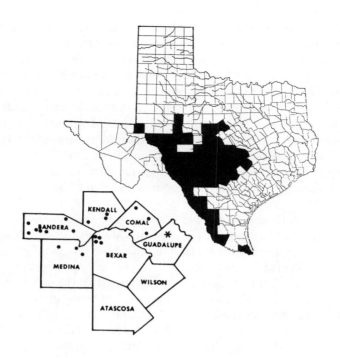

EASTERN TREE LIZARD

Urosaurus ornatus ornatus (Baird and Girard) 1852

The tree lizard genus *Urosaurus* is represented in South Central Texas by the eastern tree lizard *U. o. ornatus,* a relatively small member of the family Iguanidae. *Urosaurus ornatus* ranges from the Edwards Plateau, west through the southwestern deserts and mountains to southeastern California, north to southern Wyoming, and south into northern Mexico. This species thus is one of the most widespread and common of North American lizards. It is primarily arboreal or semi-arboreal in the South Central Texas area and is active during the day-light hours. This lizard is decorated with dark spots and bars on a gray-ish-brown background, providing a good camouflage against lichen-covered rocks or tree trunks.

Identification: The dorsal ground color is usually light grayish brown and is marked with dark, irregular blotches or crossbands. Some of these blotches may be edged with a light blue color. There are several small, distinct dark stripes and a few pale blotches on the head and legs. Females may have an orange and white spot on the white throat, and the ventral surface is missing the blue patches normally seen in the male. Male tree lizards usually have a vivid blue or blue-green area on the middle of the throat, and blue-colored ventral patches on the undersurface. *Small, granular dorsal scales, variable in size,* are characteristic of the genus, and usually the middorsal linear scale rows are much larger than the others. These larger scales are arranged in even rows and are divided into two parallel rows on either side of the median line by a series of smaller, keeled vertebral scales less than one-half the size of the largest dorsals. The head scales are relatively large in comparison to the trunk dorsal scales, and the frontal scale on top of the head is transversely divided. A faint, wrinkled lateral fold can be found along either side of the body, and *a fold of skin is located running across the underside of the throat.* Other general characteristics for identification include a tail less than twice the length of the head and body length, femoral pores that average 10 to 13, and enlarged postanal scales present in males.

This widespread species may be mistaken for several other similar species on the Edwards Plateau. These include various members of the genus *Sceloporus,* such as the rosebelly lizard (*S. variabilis marmoratus*), southern prairie lizard (*S. undulatus consobrinus*), Texas spiny lizard (*S. olivaceus*), and the crevice spiny lizard (*S. poinsettii poinsettii*). These species are distinguished from the eastern tree lizard (*Urosaurus ornatus ornatus*) by lacking a complete fold across the throat and by having scales which are approximately all the same size across the dorsal surface.

The plateau earless lizard (*Holbrookia lacerata lacerata*) can be distinguished from the eastern tree lizard by the absence of visible ear membranes.

Size: Adults reach maturity at approximately $4^{1}/_{2}$ inches (11.4 cm) in total length, and large adults may reach $6^{1}/_{4}$ inches (15.9 cm).

Behavior: The male is highly territorial and will challenge a trespassing member of its own species in its home range territory. This behavioral display usually involves push-ups on all four legs, exposing itself sideways to the intruder, laterally compressing its body, and extending its dewlap. This confrontational behavior gives an intruder the option of challenging or withdrawing, and usually lasts only a few minutes. If the intruder withdraws, the male resident may chase it from the territory or climb to a lookout post on a rock or tree while the intruder withdraws. Females of this species appear not to participate in territorial defense as males do. These quick-moving lizards, when observed in the field, often indulge in bobbing movements as they move from one rock or tree to another. They are elusive, found in pairs or small groups, and usually rest in a vertical position.

Food: The diet includes an extensive range of insects and other soft-bodied (mostly terrestrial) arthropods, including some spiders captured during early morning or late afternoon foraging.

Habitat: This lizard appears to be moderately common along open bottom washes of canyons near water and along boulders or rimrock areas in arid regions where they can take refuge in crevices. They are not restricted to this type of habitat, however, and may be common in association with oak, juniper, or mesquite trees, as well as stumps, bushes, fence posts, and buildings. The eastern tree lizard is not normally found south or east of the Balcones Escarpment in South Central Texas, with the exception of a single occurrence from northern Guadalupe County.

Breeding: The likely reproductive season for *U. ornatus* on the Edwards Plateau of South Central Texas begins in March and extends through August, with ovulation for females beginning in April. This oviparous subspecies possesses a multiple clutch potential, laying 3 clutches of eggs per season (Martin, 1973), with an average of 5 or 6 eggs per clutch. The clutch size is normally larger earlier in the egg-laying season. For example, a female may average 6 eggs in her first clutch (usually laid in May), 4 or 5 eggs in the second clutch (late June or early July), and still have sufficient time available for a possible third clutch (early August) with an average of 5 or 6 eggs per clutch. Hatchlings usually measure 1¼ to 1¾ inches (32 to 44 mm) in total length at birth. These hatchlings are usually observed in South Central Texas beginning in late June. Sexual maturity is achieved in approximately 10 or 11 months. Males of this species, along with many other lizard species, may mate with more than one female during the breeding season.

General information: The word *ornatus* is Latin, and refers to ornament or decoration.

Skinks
(Family — Scincidae)

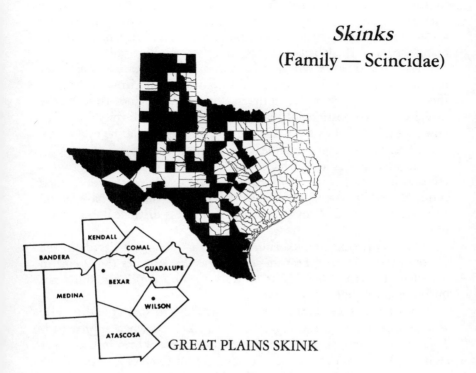

GREAT PLAINS SKINK

Eumeces obsoletus (Baird and Girard) 1852

The skink genus *Eumeces* of the cosmopolitan family Scincidae, is widely distributed throughout the Northern Hemisphere. The great plains skink is one of the 12 species of *Eumeces* in the United States. It ranges from the grassland plains of southern Nebraska, south to the state of Tamaulipas in Mexico, and west to the semiarid environments of mountains, mesas, and canyons in central Arizona. It is seldom encountered in South Central Texas, with most sightings in Kerr County on the Edwards Plateau and south of the Nueces River in South Texas. Additionally, there are isolated records for Helotes and Sutherland Springs.

Identification: The adult dorsal ground color varies from a pale olive to tan or olive-brown to gray with irregular black or dark brown markings on the edges of the scales. Occasionally, the dark markings on the edges of the scales may be reduced or absent on all or part of the dorsal surface, forming a light median area. The head and ventral surfaces, which are pale yellow, are relatively unmarked. *Juveniles are uniform black over the dorsal surface,* dark gray on the ventral surface, have brilliant white and orange spots on the labials and face, and possess a blue tail.

This lizard has *smooth, rounded shiny scales arranged in diagonal scale rows* on the sides of the body, usually converging horizontally toward the upper dorsal surface. Other diagnostic features include the presence (usually) of two postmental scales on the underside of the chin, window-like lower eyelids to enable the lizard to see while the eyelids are closed, relatively strong small legs, and a stout body.

Similar species in South Central Texas, such as the smaller southern prairie skink (*Eumeces septentrionalis obtusirostris*) and the short-lined skink (*Eumeces tetragrammus brevilineatus*), differ in that they have lateral body scales in parallel rows, and usually possess distinct dorsal striping.

Size: This stout-bodied skink is one of the largest lizards in the United States. It may measure as much as 13¾ inches (34.9 cm) in total length, with 10- to 12-inch (25.4 to 30.5 cm) long adults not uncommon throughout their range.

Behavior: These skinks prefer to stay close to shelter and usually will disappear into dense vegetation or rock cliffs when approached. This diurnal lizard is usually active during temperatures in the upper eighties (30 C.) to the middle nineties (35 C.). Fitch (1955) described how he cautiously followed several individuals for as much as 50 feet (18 m), and noticed that they always stayed close to the rock cliffs and similar shelters that were well-screened by dense vegetation. They usually attempt to bite when captured, and the bite can be painful. These are mostly secretive lizards, and a captive great plains skink will not hesitate to excavate a burrow in loose soil for concealment. Burrows found under rocks might wind around with lateral branches or enter and exit in a relatively straight course. Even though the home range is ill-defined in this species, Fitch (1955) found that lizards living within their preferred habitat usually stayed within an area roughly 10 to 200 feet (3.6 to 72.9 m) across, with a mean movement of about 40 feet (14.6 m), and that males moved farther than females and juveniles. Moreover, some lizards spent several days in their burrow under the same flat rock, only to emerge briefly and return. These shelters appeared to be occupied only for days or weeks as the skink moved on to another site, often several yards away. Additionally, Sarratt (pers.

comm.) and Hutchinson (1986) reported that they occasionally found this lizard crossing the roads in South Texas at night.

Food: The diet for this skink is known to include crickets, grasshoppers, leafhoppers, caterpillars, arachnids, centipedes, snails, and other small invertebrates. Small lizards, such as the juvenile collared lizards (*Crotaphytus collaris*), have been reported in their diet, but, according to other sources, vertebrate lizards of other species are usually left alone when kept in the same cage with the great plains skink. According to Axtell (pers. comm.), however, they will investigate and eat just about anything that moves.

Habitat: This primarily grassland species is found over a wide geographic range from mixed woodlands and prairies to desert habitats, often in association with rocks, logs, boards, and stands of short thick grass. This skink prefers soils that are suitable for burrowing, usually in association with large flat rocks along slopes that it uses for shelter. Other common habitat sites include open hillsides with scattered flat rocks, limestone ledges or outcrops, and low rolling hills covered with grama and bluestem grasses, moist floodplains, and sparsely wooded pastureland, usually near an intermittent or permanent water supply.

Breeding: The mating season usually starts in April and continues through June. Although 7 to 24 eggs per clutch have been reported in this species, the average clutch size appears to be 11 or 12. The eggs are laid in late May through July in deep moist burrows, usually beneath large objects such as rocks. Females may remain with the eggs after they are laid. The white eggs measure $3/4$ to $7/8$ inch (19 to 22 mm) by $7/16$ to $9/16$ inch (12 to 15 mm). Hatchlings, $2^{1}/2$ to $3^{1}/16$ inches (64 to 78 mm) in length, first appear in late June, July, and August. There is some speculation that sexual maturity may be obtained by some South Texas females in two years, but a majority of the females studied in Kansas, according to Fitch (1955), were found to have maturing ova at approximately 3 years of age.

General information: Predators of this skink include hawks, opossums, moles, spotted skunks, striped skunks, and one account of a collared lizard. Damaged and regenerated tails are very common among large adults, as only about one in four adult lizards has its original tail.

This skink will change color and pattern substantially as it grows from juvenile to adult, and this should be taken into account when identifying small individuals.

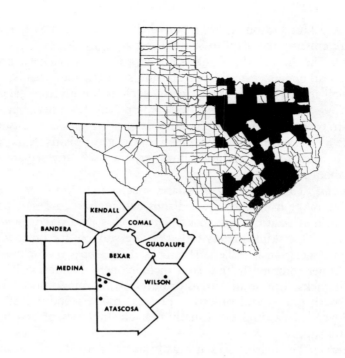

SOUTHERN PRAIRIE SKINK

Eumeces septentrionalis obtusirostris Bocourt 1879

This species of skink is associated with the tall-grass prairies of central North America from southern Canada to Central Texas. There are two subspecies; *Eumeces septentionalis obtusirostris,* occurring from south-central Kansas and down to South Central Texas, and then eastward to the Coastal Bend area.

Identification: The southern prairie skink has rather striking differences in pattern and color between eastern and western populations in Texas, as pointed out by Smith and Slater (1949); these are seldom recognized as distinct entities. This highly variable skink has *a dark lateral stripe on each side of the body, usually bordered by a light lateral line, and above by a light dorsolateral line. This stripe system (especially the dark stripe) extends down the length of the body and onto the tail. The light lateral line passes above the ear membrane.* A dark border may be present above the

66

dorsolateral light line, and a dark-bordered median light line is occasionally present.

Hatchlings are predominantly black dorsally, including about one-third of the proximal tail, except for light mottling on the forepart and side of the head. Juveniles may have 4 or 5 light dorsal lines; the median longitudinal line usually discontinuous and occasionally missing. There is a dark area from the eye back, on the side of the head, with a very narrow, light line from in front of the eye to above the ear; this line may become broken as it continues back onto the body. The posterior two-thirds of the tail is bright blue.

The adult ventral surface is relatively unmarked, and a pale cream color is found under the throat. During the mating season in the spring, males often develop a bright salmon-orange color on the jaws. This lizard has smooth, shiny scales which are in parallel rows (except on the sides for some lizards) with short, well-developed limbs that do not overlap or touch when the limbs are adpressed, i.e., when the forelimb is extended backward along the body and the hind limb is brought fully forward.

Other characteristics include seven lower labial scales, absence of a postnasal scale, and two postmental scales found under the chin. Adult males tend to have larger heads than females.

Similar species include the short-lined skink (*Eumeces tetragrammus brevilineatus*), which differs because its light stripes end at the shoulder and do not extend to the tail, and the ground skink (*Scincella lateralis*), which is distinguished by its small adult size and lack of distinct light stripes.

Size: Measurements recorded for this species range from approximately 5 to $8^{1}/_{8}$ inches (12.7 to 20.7 cm), maximum, in total length.

Behavior: This terrestrial skink is rarely encountered, perhaps because of its reported twilight and early morning activity pattern. Southern prairie skinks may emerge in South Central Texas during late March, according to Axtell (pers. comm.). Like many other lizards, if disturbed by an intruder it will seek refuge under logs, boards, flat rocks, or in burrows.

Food: The diet consists primarily of insects, spiders, and other arthropods, and invertebrates like snails.

Habitat: This lizard often hides in the loose earth under large masses of roots of the common prickly pear cactus, often entering small burrows under the roots. It also has been reported to be found near water, under piles of dead leaves, decaying logs, flat boards, tar paper, old tin, and debris near heavy vegetation in slightly moist, well-drained, sandy areas of Wilson County, west to northwest Atascosa County, and north to Somerset, Texas, in Bexar County. The southern prairie skink, according to the author's numerous inquiries and personal records, has not been observed in northwest Atascosa County in years. However, no extensive field observations have been conducted in that area since A. J. Kirn collected there prior to 1950. Axtell, however, found this species still extant in Wilson County in the early 1980s.

Breeding: The reproductive habits of this species in South Central Texas are not well-known. Mating in this region of Texas may start in late March or April. J. E. Johnson, Jr., reported eggs being laid on top of the soil in a small S-shaped trench about 1-inch (25 mm) wide, 6 inches (15.2 cm) long, and 1½ inches (38 mm) deep, with a small hole extending into the sand as an escape exit for the brooding female (Smith and Slater, 1949). The number of eggs laid by this species apparently varies geographically. The average number of eggs laid is from 5 to 18, whereas Fitch (1985) reported an 11.7 mean clutch size for *E. septentrionalis* in the central portion of the southern United States. This and other *Eumeces* species produce only one clutch of eggs annually.

General information: Information about the life history and habits of this secretive species is extremely limited.

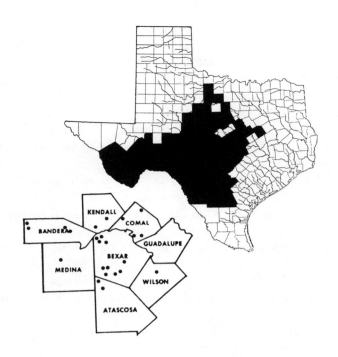

SHORT-LINED SKINK

Eumeces tetragrammus brevilineatus Cope 1880

This relatively common skink is found over most of South Central Texas, although none have yet been documented in Guadalupe County to the east. The species is widely distributed in the southwestern U.S. and northern Mexico, and this subspecies is found from South Central Texas, north to Baylor County, and west to the Big Bend country, and then south to Coahuila and Nuevo Leon, Mexico.

Identification: The dorsal ground color varies in adults from olive-brown or greenish-gray to gray, with or without dark edges on the dorsal scales. Two light-colored stripes are found above and below each eye, extending backward across the side of the head and neck, usually terminating in the region of the shoulder or, occasionally, at about mid-body. Breeding males have an orange color on the sides of the upper and lower labials and sides of the throat. Juveniles have a bright metallic blue tail. Ventrally, adults are dusky cream-colored on the chin and chest region, with the remainder of the underside a bluish hue. Young may be considerably darker than adults. The juvenile dorsal ground color is a deep chocolate-brown. The sharply defined, cream-colored, dorsolateral lines extend backward from the tip of the snout, passing above each nostril and across the supraoculars, and then disappearing well behind the axilla. Complete pattern loss may occur in very large or old individuals.

Similar species in South Central Texas include the southern prairie skink (*Eumeces septentrionalis obtusirostris*), which differs by having two light dorsolateral lines extending from the neck to the basal portion of the tail area, and the ground skink (*Scincella lateralis*), which may be distinguished by its small adult size and absence of distinct light striping. Moreover, very old individuals of both these species tend not to lose all traces of pattern (especially the dark lateral stripe), whereas completely patternless individuals of short-lined skinks occasionally occur.

Size: The average adult size recorded for this subspecies ranges from 5 to 7$\frac{1}{8}$ inches (12.7 to 18.1 cm) in length.

Behavior: Short-lined skinks are active during daylight hours. Foraging activities during the day through leaf litter in search of insects is a major part of this lizard's daily activity.

Food: The diet consists chiefly of small insects and other arthropods, including spiders.

Habitat: This lizard is most abundant in relatively dry wooded uplands and woodlands in association with rocky areas. It is also found in grasslands and brushlands with sandy soil, in riparian woodlands, and near springs and seepage slopes.

The short-lined skink (*Eumeces tetragrammus brevilineatus*) intergrades with the four-lined skink (*Eumeces tetragrammus tetragrammus*) in southern Texas, usually in the vicinity of the Nueces River drainage system. This area ranges along the Nueces River from the Live Oak County region of the Nueces River, west, and then north to the edge of the Edwards Plateau.

Breeding: Reproductive data on this lizard are limited. Females are reported to lay from 5 to 17 eggs, although 8 to 10 eggs per clutch is the documented average. These nongranular and nonadhesive eggs average $^7/_{16}$-inch (11 mm) by $^5/_{16}$-inch (8 mm). Most short-lined skinks are reported to lay their eggs in May, with the first 2-inch (5.1 cm) long hatchlings appearing in June.

General information: The type locality for this subspecies is Helotes in Bexar County, and original syntypes were collected by Gabriel Marnock.

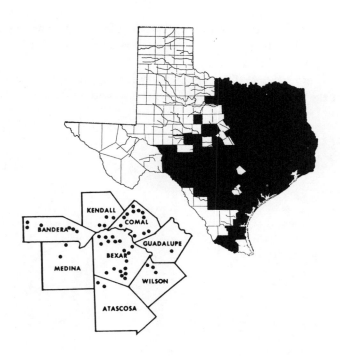

GROUND SKINK

Scincella lateralis (Say) 1823

The ground skink is one of the most abundant lizards in South Central Texas. This small, slender-bodied skink has short legs and a long tail. *Scincella lateralis* is found over most of the eastern and southern United States, from the Atlantic coast of southern New Jersey, to the Florida Keys, west to eastern and south-central Kansas, Oklahoma, and south to the Texas Gulf Coast.

Identification: This shiny, smooth-scaled lizard is a variable reddish-chocolate, copper, to golden-brown color dorsally, with a broad, dark dorsolateral stripe on each side extending from the tip of the snout through the eye and continuing back onto the tail. The light ventro-lateral color is occasionally peppered with a darker brown, and the ventral surface is usually whitish or yellowish in color. The head and tail surfaces usually are the same color as the upper dorsal shade of brown, and in dark specimens

72

it is often difficult to distinguish the dark lateral stripe from the general ground color. Juveniles appear much like adults, having a bright copper dorsal color that fades on the neck to a light brown. Other characteristics include a pair of scales behind the frontal scale, one median frontonasal contacting the rostral scale, and a transparent disk window in the lower eyelid allowing the skink to see when the eye is closed. This lizard has short and weak limbs. When the forelimb is laid backward along the body and the hind limb is brought forward at full length, they are separated by about 10 to 20 scales.

Similar species in South Central Texas include the southern prairie skink (*Eumeces septentrionalis obtusirostris*), which has two light dorsolateral lines that extend from the neck to the tail on each side, and the short-lined skink (*Eumeces tetragrammus brevilineatus*), with paired dorsolateral light stripes ending at the shoulder area. Both these species of *Eumeces* are larger in overall size than the ground skink.

Size: The ground skink is a relatively small skink, only ranging from about 3 to 5 1/8 inches (7.7 to 13.1 cm) in total length.

Behavior: This species is relatively secretive, usually seeking thick ground cover and rarely venturing far out onto open ground. Hibernation of this species is limited to the coldest days of winter, as on many other winter days it will become active on warmer afternoons. The short limbs are used in slow locomotion, and are less important than lateral serpentine movements during rapid movements. Territorial disputes may occur when males are placed in the same enclosure (Lewis, 1951). The skink may flex its neck in the direction of the other skink, and the tail may be lashed in an irregular and violent manner.

This species is usually very active during the daylight hours and is quite agile in escaping potential predators. The author has also observed these lizards climbing up the bark of large trees when cornered. Lewis (1951) reported cannibalism when small juveniles were kept in a cage with adults. One, a large female, consumed five newly hatched young that were not her own. Mather (1970) reported that this skink's activity pattern appeared to be associated with moisture and soil temperature, with the maximum activity being recorded between 65 and 70 F. (18 and 21 C.) during non-drought conditions. Brooks (1967) reported significant activity at a higher temperature of 75 to 82 F. (25 to 30 C.). Mather (1970) noted, with limited data, that the average distance between recaptured male skinks was 34 feet (12.4 m) and between recaptured females was about 22.8 feet (8.3 m). Brooks (1967) found the average size of a home range, determined from the records of 16 males (captured 8 or more times during a 12-month period), was 62 square yards, with a range of 30 to 127. The average size of a home range, determined from the records of 36 females (captured 5 or more times during the same period), was 17 square yards with a range of 3 to 67.

Food: The diet usually consists of a variety of small arthropods, with apparent preference for roaches, leafhoppers, Diptera, and moths. Other invertebrates recorded in their diet include isopods, maggots, mealworms, pupae of other insects, small arachnids, and amphipod crustaceans.

Habitat: This forest-floor inhabitant is often found foraging among deep leaf litter and low-lying decaying timber. It also frequents woodland edges, especially where there is a thick layer of decaying leaves or other ground cover. They generally prefer partly shaded, moist environments, and thus tend to be found near streams. Occasionally, however, these lizards appear in yards, gardens, and open fields.

Breeding: Mating may occur from early spring through the summer, although Brooks (1967) reported follicles increased fourfold in diameter between early February and April in females from a Florida population. Females in South Central Texas may produce at least 4 clutches of eggs from April through August, and possibly into September. An average of 3 eggs per clutch is usually laid, although an average of 1 to 7 eggs has been documented. The number of eggs per clutch is positively correlated to the size of the female; the larger females usually produce larger clutches. The leathery eggs are $3/8$ inch (10 mm) by just over $3/16$ inch (5 mm) and are generally a creamy, dull white color with a faint peach tint. The female apparently leaves the nest soon after laying eggs. Hatchlings average from $1^{11}/16$ to $1^3/4$ inches (4.3 to 4.5 cm) long at birth. Sexual maturity is attained in the first year (Fitch, 1985).

General information: Observed predators include the ring-necked snake, black racer, corn snake, and southern copperhead, although doubtlessly many other carnivorous vertebrates make opportunistic use of this ubiquitous lizard.

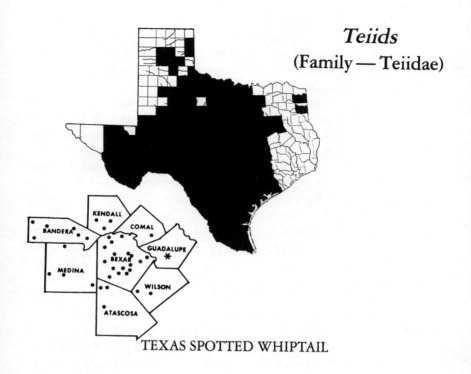

Teiids
(Family — Teiidae)

TEXAS SPOTTED WHIPTAIL

Cnemidophorus gularis gularis Baird and Girard 1852

The Texas spotted whiptail is a member of the New World family Teiidae, represented by 40 genera and about 225 to 230 species throughout the Americas. The genus *Cnemidophorus* includes approximately 44 species, several of which are unisexual and thus reproduce parthenogenetically (without fertilization of the eggs by a male). The two species in the South Central Texas area, however, are both bisexual (both males and females present). *Cnemidophorus gularis gularis* is found from southern Oklahoma through much of the Texas Panhandle south to northern Veracruz in Mexico.

Identification: This is a striped and spotted, greenish to brown-colored lizard with seven or eight, light, uninterrupted stripes extending the length of the body onto the tail, with pronounced small round spots in the dark lateral fields between the stripes. These spots are usually faint on the brightly

75

striped juveniles, and may be faint or absent below the paravertebral stripes in adults. The vertebral stripe is broad, often split into two poorly defined lines and producing an occasional "eight-stripe" appearance. The light dorsal stripes range in color from yellowish and whitish to brownish and greenish over different parts of the dorsum. *Adult coloration of the tail dorsally is a pale orange-brown, and cream ventrally.* The tail dorsum in juveniles is pinkish-red.

Males have a pink to reddish chin and throat and a bluish-black chest. The abdomen is often marked with a large, dark, marine-blue area with some black occasionally suffused with a cream color. Ventrally, females are uniform pale cream to whitish throughout life.

Other identifying characteristics include tiny, rounded dorsal scales, and several enlarged scales along the bottom edge of the throat (gular fold) and along the rear of the forearm. These are noticeably larger than the other surrounding scales. This lizard has a pointed head, a long tail which may be 2 to 3 times the snout-vent (body) length, and 8 lengthwise rows of large rectangular ventral scales. The anal plate is divided by small scales (occasionally 4 scales are present), and the number of femoral pores ranges from 14 to 20.

The southern prairie skink (*Eumeces septentrionalis obtusirostris*) has large, shiny scales of similar size going all the way around the body. The only other lizard in South Central Texas that could be confused with this lizard is the prairie-lined racerunner (*Cnemidophorus sexlineatus sexlineatus x viridis*), which differs in lacking dorsolateral light spots between the light stripes.

Size: The maximum size recorded for the Texas spotted whiptail is 12½ inches (31.8 cm) in total length (Smith and Brodie, 1982).

Behavior: This long-tailed, strong-legged lizard has been clocked at speeds up to 18 miles per hour. When not running away, this diurnal lizard is otherwise deliberate in its movements. If approached by an intruder, the lizard thus may run for a short distance and then stop to survey the surroundings before resuming its typically abrupt, jerky movements. Another interesting character of this lizard species is the rapidly moving tongue.

As this species forages for food, it will dig and move dry leaves and loose sand to find hidden invertebrate prey. This species may spend several minutes examining every twig and small stone around the base of a bush. Such foraging activities are influenced by fluctuations in temperature; cool air temperature will cause these lizards to seek refuge before the soil temperature has dropped substantially. This species thermoregulates by basking in the sun during the time periods when the soil temperature is cool, and, when the soil temperature becomes hot, it will actively seek a shaded area. Ferguson (pers. comm.) reports that they forage mainly before early afternoon; they have been recorded foraging at a 106 F. (41 C.) ground temperature.

When disturbed or seized, *Cnemidophorus gularis* occasionally emit a short, high-pitched, monosyllabic squeak (Vance, 1984). These lizards have been found hibernating in February along a moderately sloping embankment along a highway (Trauth, 1983) and in cavities under rocks. One was found in December under about 10 inches (25.4 cm) of sand in a small drift at the upper end of a ledge along a south-facing bluff near a river. Milstead (1961) calculated the minimum home range at 0.25 acres and the maximum at 0.43 acres.

Food: The diet consists of terrestrial arthropods which include termites, moth larvae, grasshoppers, beetles, ticks, and spiders. Strecker (1928) noted that large *Cnemidophorus gularis* males attacked other species of lizards, and he found a young *Cophosaurus texanus* in one of their stomachs.

Habitat: This lizard frequents a wide variety of dry habitats, including open prairie brushlands, flat brushy canyon bottoms, shrubby savannas, eroded slopes, pastures, field edges, gravel pits, and overgrown city lots. It is tolerant of a wide variety of substrate types throughout its range. Off the Edwards Plateau, however, it is primarily associated with dense soils, whereas on the Plateau proper it is also often encountered foraging in dry, water-deposited sands or silts along watercourses and near cattle tanks. Burrows beneath bushes and rocks are typical overnight refugia following daily activity.

Breeding: Reproduction for this bisexual, oviparous species begins in late April and terminates in late July, with the male's testicular activity closely paralleling this season of female ovarian productivity. Some females may mature in 10 to 12 months, probably producing a single clutch of 3 or 4 eggs in the first reproductive season. Ballinger and Schrank (1972) found an average of 4.5 eggs in 154 females near San Angelo, Texas. Many females do not mature until their second reproductive season. Older females normally produce 2 clutches of eggs per year and approximately 6 to 8 eggs per clutch (Trauth, pers. comm.). These whitish eggs usually measure $^{11}/_{16}$ (17.8 mm) by $^{1}/_{2}$ inch (12 mm). According to Trauth (1987) this species lacks the rigid, tunnel-like nest construction typically found for the racerunner *C. sexlineatus*. Moreover, the Texas spotted whiptail covers its eggs with soil, whereas *C. sexlineatus* does not. Hatchlings emerge in late spring through the first part of the summer and usually average about 4 inches (10.2 cm) in total length.

General information: Documented predators include the roadrunner, badger, coachwhip, whipsnake, and night snake.

Sex can be determined in *Cnemidophorus* by the larger femoral pores in males.

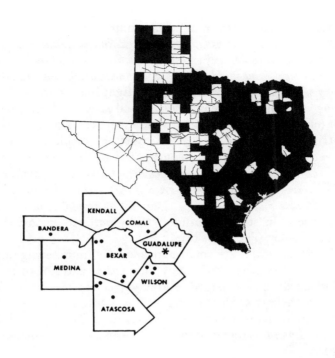

PRAIRIE-LINED RACERUNNER

Cnemidophorus sexlineatus sexlineatus (Linnaeus)
1766 x *sexlineatus viridis* Lowe 1966

    This teiid lizard, the racerunner, is the eastern and northernmost representative of the genus *Cnemidophorus* in the United States. It is found from Maryland, south to the Florida Keys, then northwest to Minnesota and Wisconsin, down the Mississippi River Valley, and southwest to at least South Texas. There is a wide area of intergradation between the six-lined racerunner (*Cnemidophorus sexlineatus sexlineatus*) and the prairie-lined racerunner (*Cnemidophorus sexlineatus viridis*) in the eastern and central sections of the state (Trauth, pers. comm.). What appears to be a lizard with some mixed characteristics from both subspecies is found south of San Antonio in the Carrizo Sand Formation. According to Trauth (1980), the lateral supraocular granule scale count of 17 to 28 places at least some of the Atascosa and

79

Comal County lizards into an intergrade status.

Identification: Adults usually have six distinct, longitudinal, white to yellowish, narrow lines dorsally extending from the head onto the tail. A narrow and extremely faint middorsal stripe, approximately three granule scales wide, may be present. The area between the light lines is greenish or very dark gray in color, with the bottom lateral stripe blending with the whitish (or in males, blue-tinged) ventral surface. The median dorsal light stripes are obscure on the tail, but the dorsolateral ones may clearly extend down most of its length, bordered below by a dark line. *Females tend to have a whitish or salmon throat and ventral surface, while males may have a pale blue or blue-green throat and cheek with a creamy, washed with pale blue, ventral area.* Hatchlings resemble adults generally, but the light stripes are more vividly outlined against the very dark ground color. The tail is bright blue.

The dorsal scales are small and granular, numbering approximately 72 to 104 around midbody, and scales anterior to the deep gular fold are abruptly enlarged. Postantebrachial scales on the back of the forearm are only slightly enlarged in this lizard. There are 8 rows of large, rectangular scales on the ventral surface. The long and slender tail of *C. sexlineatus* is rough to the touch. Femoral pores number about 23 to 40.

The only similar species in South Central Texas is the Texas spotted whiptail (Cnemidophorus gularis gularis), usually found on denser soils and readily distinguished by the small, round, pale spots in the dorsolateral dark fields between the light lines. Skinks, which are also longitudinally striped, have large, shiny dorsal scales of the same size dorsally and ventrally.

Size: Sexually mature adults average approximately 5½ to 9½ inches (14.0 to 24.2 cm) in total length, with females tending to be slightly larger in body size than males.

Behavior: During hot weather this diurnal lizard is most active during the morning, although daily and seasonal activities vary. According to Paulissen (1988) it has a field activity body temperature of 101 to 102 F. (38.1 to 38.5 C.). Although a high air temperature may influence this lizard's foraging activities, the soil temperature is also important. *C. sexlineatus* emerges in April in South Central Texas as diurnal temperatures climb. This species' lower temperature limit is relatively high, limiting or terminating its activity outside its burrow from November to April. Clark (1976) estimated the home range of 39 six-lined racerunners at Texas A&M Research Annex in Brazos County.

The home range size was similar for males and females, and averaged 13,099 square meters. When males decreased in density, their home range significantly increased in size. Moreover, there is a tendency in this species to prefer one part of its home range over another, and to occasionally relocate its entire home range.

The six-lined racerunner is well-equipped for digging into the sandy soil found south of San Antonio, having forelimbs with long claws that allow it to construct burrows for shelter and protection. Foraging involves jerky, probing movements with the snout beneath objects and into crevices or holes. These lizards depend more on sight and less on scent than some other lizard species in locating their prey (H. Smith, pers. comm.).

Food: Recorded food items include small insects like planthoppers, leafhoppers, grasshoppers, crickets, adult moths, caterpillars, true bugs, beetles, wasps, and occasionally ants and flies. Spiders also make up a large percentage of their diet, with an occasional snail taken (Paulissen, 1987).

Habitat: In South Central Texas this lizard primarily occurs in the open areas of post oak woodland along the Carrizo Sand Formation in Guadalupe, Wilson, Atascosa, and southern Bexar counties. Here it is found in dry, open wooded bottomlands, well-drained eroded areas, weedy roadsides, fence rows, sparsely vegetated open fields, sand dunes, hilly habitats, and margins of thickets. Analysis of a southern Oklahoma population indicated that juveniles used more exposed microhabitats than did adults during most of the year (probably due to large lizards being at greater risk of overheating in exposed microhabitats) (Paulissen, 1988).

The Carrizo Sand areas support the best regional populations, but this species has been also documented from the Cibolo River bottom in Wilson County, and Strecker reported one from the eastern part of Kendall County near the Comal County line. Literature records indicate its occurrence in Bandera, Comal, and Medina counties, but this author has not been able to verify any of these Edwards Plateau records.

Breeding: Copulation begins in late April, a few weeks after emergence from hibernation in early April or possibly late March. Mating involves the male grasping the female with a dorsal neck grip, short body jerks, hindquarter movements, then arching his body about her hindquarters to effect intromission. Copulation may last for a few minutes. Gravid females start laying their eggs in May and again in late June or July, although gravid females have been observed in August. Intervals between the female egg clutches usually average 45 days, with Carpenter (1960) reporting a mean incubation period of 53 days in Oklahoma. Egg-laying data indicate that *C. sexlineatus* can produce at least 2 clutches of eggs per season (Clark, 1976). Six eggs have been reported in a clutch composite (possibly 2 clutches) by Cook (1943), but the average is approximately 3 eggs per clutch, often depending on such nongeographic factors as the size and age of the female (Fitch, 1985; Trauth, 1983). Most males and females attain sexual maturity in time to reproduce at one year of age (Clark, 1976). Eggs enlarge after they are laid, from $5/8$ inch (16.2 mm) by $5/16$ inch (9.3 mm) to approximately $11/16$ inch (18.4 mm) by $1/2$ inch (13 mm) at hatching (Fitch, 1958).

Six-lined racerunners may dig a nest cavity into a well-drained, moist zone of sand, approximately 3 to 11 inches (7.7 to 28.0 cm) in depth and about three times the size of the enclosed eggs (Brown, 1956). Hatchlings range from $3 1/2$ to $3 5/8$ inches (8.9 to 9.3 cm) in length at birth.

General information: Racerunners have been found in stomachs of kingsnakes such as *Lampropeltis getulus* and *Lampropeltis calligaster,* eastern hognose snakes (*Heterodon platyrhinos*), and the western coachwhip (*Masticophis flagellum*). Other predators include hawks, roadrunners, skunks, coyotes, and armadillos.

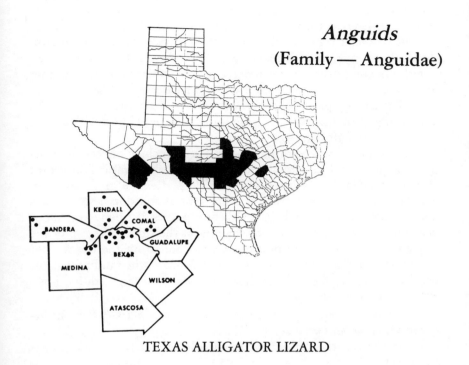

Anguids
(Family — Anguidae)

TEXAS ALLIGATOR LIZARD

Gerrhonotus liocephalus infernalis Baird 1858

The Texas alligator lizard belongs to the family Anguidae, a relatively small family of about a dozen genera occurring mostly in the temperate and subtropical regions of the Northern Hemisphere, but also includes tropical forms. Although taxonomy of the genus *Gerrhonotus* is somewhat unsettled at present, the generic name has been historically applied to those lizards in the family with the "alligator lizard" body form, including a stiff-looking body, large plate-like scales, and a fairly large, triangular head.

Gerrhonotus liocephalus inhabits much of the Sierra Madre of Mexico and is composed of several subspecies. The subspecies *G. l. infernalis* is found from the Edwards Plateau of Texas, west through the Big Bend, and south to San Luis Potosi in Mexico.

Identification: The adult dorsal color pattern ranges from tan to light

83

brown with seven to nine, light-edged, irregular, dark crossbands on the body, and several more on the tail. Juveniles are more distinctly marked than adults, with vivid white and dark brown to black crossbands being present. Large or very old adults may lose all traces of pattern, and individuals of any size with regenerated tails show only a uniform yellowish-tan color in the regrown portion. The elongated head and front legs are unmarked, whereas the back legs have some indistinct markings. The iris is typically light gray in color. Ventral scales are smooth and arranged in 12 rows, the pale undersurface being mottled with white, tan, and gray flecks.

Important distinguishing characteristics include plate-like dorsal scales and a flap-like lateral groove between the armpit and groin. When extended during breathing, this deep, flexible groove will reveal granular scales between the larger ventral and dorsal scales. The dorsal scales are arranged in 16 rows, the top rows distinctly keeled but becoming only faintly keeled to smooth on the sides. The top of the snout has a small median postrostral scale bordering the rostral. Ear membranes are large and obvious on this lizard. When unbroken, the prehensile tail is much longer than the body. Few large adults, however, possess complete tails.

The distinct body shape and lateral groove make it unlikely that this lizard would be confused with any other species.

Size: This is the largest lizard in South Central Texas. It measures from 10 to 17 inches (25.4 to 43.1 cm) from the snout to the tip of the tail. The record reported length is 20 inches (50.8 cm). This specimen had a snout-vent length of 8 inches (20.4 cm).

Behavior: Compared to many lizards, Texas alligator lizards appear to prefer cooler temperatures and thus could be active on a year-round basis in the South Central Texas area. Several lizards have been observed moving or sunning themselves in the winter months. In January 1987 a female was taken near Helotes, Texas, with the daytime temperature at only 45 F. (7.5 C.). Werler (1949) reported a female taken in Bexar County on February 28, 1949. Flury (1949) reported an individual sunning itself on a warm December day, and another was found on a cliff near Canyon Dam in February 1971 at about 55 F. (12.5 C.). There is an indication that this lizard may be more active during spring and fall, although many of the author's records indicate specimens being found consistently on midsummer mornings. Lizards were found occasionally after light showers in the morning or near water during midsummer. The author has observed two specimens which came out onto the gravel roads of the less-populated parts of the Edwards Plateau on an overcast afternoon and the early twilight of a late summer day. When not moving around, however, they seem to favor perches in the tangled, bare branches of the upper parts of fallen juniper or other small trees. This diurnal lizard is characterized by slow, deliberate movements and generally is mild-mannered if captured. It is capable of inflicting a powerful pinching bite which, although painful, contains no poison or venom. These lizards have tail vertebrae, each with a fracture plane where the tail can readily be detached, leaving the tail wriggling in the predator's mouth or on the ground as the lizard crawls to safety. The tail is slightly prehensile. When foraging for food, this lizard will slowly investigate objects with slow tongue flicks. The tail is used as a possible decoy when stalking insects (pers. obser.). When slowly stalking their food in the wild, these lizards may depend on deception to capture it. Just before seizing the prey, the body becomes rigid and is raised above the ground. The tail is curved away from the lizard's body and is vibrated just before the lizard lunges at the prey. It appears to this author that the lizard is possibly trying to distract the prey from the main section of the lizard's body. Possibly, a higher percentage of insects might jump and escape when this tactic is not used. Although these lizards are mostly solitary in their habits, the author has made five different field observations in which a male and female were together. Fighting is rare, even when competing for food. The only time this author noticed aggressive behavior was when another large male was introduced into an enclosure in which another male and female were already together. The males usually arch the back of the neck in defensive posture, but this behavior usually lasts only for a short period with no subsequent flare-up being observed. The author does agree with H. Smith (pers. comm.), who suggested that this species shows indications of learning quickly and forming habits.

Food: Included in its wide-ranging diet are insects such as crickets, various beetles and their larvae, grasshoppers, roaches, mealworms, cicadas, moths, and other slow-moving insects. Other dietary items include snails, spiders, scorpions, worms, lizards (*Eumeces obsoletus, Holbrookia texana,* and *Sceloporus*), small snakes (juvenile *Thamnophis sirtalis,* newborn *Elaphe guttata,* and adult *Storeria dekayi*), and newborn mice. Young hatchlings eat small insects, worms, and spiders.

Habitat: This handsome creature is found in oak-juniper woodlands, i.e., in breaks usually near or in bushes, and on valley slopes and

85

rocky hillsides, especially in association with streams of the Edwards Plateau and the Balcones Escarpment. Hill Country habitats in Bandera, Kendall, Comal, and Bexar counties include crevices in rocky bluffs, under flat rocks, in dry leaves along rocky hillsides, and at or near watercourses in rocky areas. In Mexico, they are often found around the bottom of large agaves.

Breeding: The Texas *Gerrhonotus* are egg-layers (oviparous). Reproductive information on the Texas alligator lizard is scarce and somewhat perplexing. The author's data, along with one literature source (Flury, 1949) and two private keepers, indicate that the Edwards Plateau alligator lizard population mates in November. The female lays 5 to 31 eggs in February, March, April, or May, although one late January and one early June oviposition have been observed. Eggs measure $3/4$ inch (19 mm) by $7/16$ inch (11 mm), as determined by averaging data from several clutches. Females will coil around their eggs after they are laid (brooding behavior). Optimum egg incubation temperatures are not yet known, although successful hatchings in captivity have occurred from 75 to 95 F. (25 to 35 C.). On three different occasions the author has observed females laying eggs in the coolest spot in the cage away from both light bulbs or hot rocks. Eggs normally hatch in late March, April, or May, and occasionally in June. They usually hatch in 43 to 49 days, with one report of 34 days. The hatchlings are $3\frac{1}{8}$ to 4 inches (8.0 to 10.2 cm) long at birth. According to limited growth records of the author, they may become sexually mature (adult snout-vent length) in their third or fourth year. Burkett (1962) reported that 2 clutches of eggs were laid in a period of just over 3 weeks (31 eggs laid on May 14, and 28 eggs on June 9). However, the author's reproductive records indicate that a captive 8-inch (20.3 cm), snout-vent length female from South Central Texas will normally lay only 28 to 31 eggs in a single clutch.

General information: The flexible lateral groove allows for the consumption of large meals, as a dozen or more insects can be consumed by a single adult in one meal. In addition, in females this groove allows extra lateral expansion room for large egg clutches.

The tongue is long and forked (somewhat snake-like). Like snakes, the alligator lizard sheds its skin in one piece.

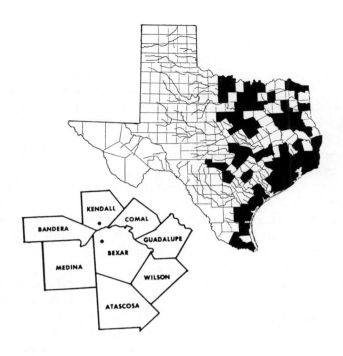

WESTERN SLENDER GLASS LIZARD

Ophisaurus attenuatus attenuatus Cope 1880

Members of the genus *Ophisaurus* are limbless except for some Old World species that have tiny hind limbs. They are members of the family Anguidae, which have scales reinforced with bony plates called osteoderms. Western slender glass lizards are often mistaken for snakes, and throughout their range they are known locally, but erroneously, as "glass snakes." However, a glass lizard is quickly distinguished from a snake by its movable eyelids, external ear membranes, and rather stiff body. The species occurs in the southeastern and east-central United States. The subspecies in Texas, the western slender glass lizard, is relatively common in eastern and coastal Texas, but it is extremely rare or extirpated in the South Central Texas area. The last known *Ophisaurus attenuatus* collected in South Central Texas was in 1913 by Louis Garni in Boerne, near the southern part of Kendall

County. According to Garni's notes, he found it early one morning among some weeds along the San Antonio and Aransas Pass railroad tracks.

Identification: *The buff or pale yellowish-tan ground color of the dorsal surface occupies scale rows one through three and the upper third of the fourth scale row. There is a darker, brownish middorsal stripe (sometimes broken into dashes), extending the length of the body and continuing for nearly three-fourths the distance of the proximal tail.* The pattern above the lateral groove usually consists of 3 dark brown (black in the young) stripes separated by two narrow yellowish to white stripes on each side (sometimes broken in older specimens). There are also narrow, dark, longitudinal stripes below the lateral groove and under the tail. Dorsal stripes tend to be interrupted near the anterior end of the lateral fold. The head pattern is mottled with brown, yellow, and white laterally. *Ophisaurus attenuatus* has broken white markings dorsally, fading posteriorly on the upper dorsum. The ventral surface is yellowish.

Other identification features include 98 to 115 scales along the lateral groove, 14 longitudinal series of dorsal scales, plate-like body scales (that may have a rounded keel), no labials reaching orbit, frontonasal usually undivided, lateral fold along each side, scales in lateral fold granular, *movable eyelids, external ear membranes,* an elongated, tapering body form, *no legs,* unregenerated tail 2.4 times the snout-vent length, and a regenerated tail that is sharply pointed and a different color from the original tail.

No other lizard in Texas resembles this one, so it can only be confused with a snake. Snakes do not have movable eyelids or external ear membranes.

Size: Adult measurements usually range from 21 to 28 inches (53.4 to 71.0 cm) from the snout to the end of the tail. The extraordinary record length (Conant, 1975) is listed at 42 inches (106.7 cm).

Behavior: The author has observed this secretive, primarily diurnal lizard foraging in the open during the day along the Texas coast on several occasions, although it has also been found in or near small brush, grass, and leaves. On February 27, 1988, at Aransas National Wildlife Refuge, a 28-inch (71.0 cm) long specimen was apparently basking on the Dagger Point hiking trail. Air temperature was approximately 65 F. (18.5 C.) and the time was about 2:30 in the afternoon. Despite the cool temperature, it moved rapidly off the trail into the low brush. Although a reportedly recently-killed individual was found on a highway in Oklahoma at 10:30 P.M. (Webb, 1970), along the Texas

88

Gulf Coast this lizard is usually diurnal. This species has been observed in late November and February in this coastal region, and may be active at somewhat lower temperatures than other lizards.

Slender glass lizards are reported to emerge after light rains, possibly in search of suitable prey items. They are good burrowers in the wild and are often found hiding beneath the surface mat of dead vegetation or underground in abandoned burrows of other animals (Fitch, 1989). If a predator attempts to grasp one, it will twist and thrash vigorously to try to escape, often detaching its tail. Not surprisingly, a substantial percentage of the larger specimens encountered have regenerated tails.

Food: The diet of this lizard includes grasshoppers, crickets, beetles, caterpillars, and other insects and their larvae; spiders, snails, small bird eggs laid in ground nests, mice, and small lizards and snakes have also been recorded (McConkey, 1954).

Habitat: This terrestrial lizard is found on loose, sandy soil primarily in dry grassland and open wooded areas around shortgrass, shrubs, decaying leaves and brush, small trees, grass along sandy fields and pastures, and occasionally, hedges in urban areas.

Breeding: Little is known about the reproduction of this species in Texas. In Arkansas they are reported to mate in April through late May (Trauth, 1984); in Kansas, they lay from 5 to 16 eggs (Fitch, 1989) in early June, July, and occasionally August. Females have been documented brooding their eggs, which usually measure $5/8$ to $3/4$ inch (16 to 20 mm) by $7/16$ to $1/2$ inch (12 to 13 mm) at deposition. At hatching, however, eggs can measure 1-inch (26 mm) by $13/16$ inch (21 mm), thus showing a considerable size increase during incubation. Hatchlings average $4^3/8$ to $5^1/8$ inches (11.2 to 13.1 cm) in total length at birth; these usually appear in July through October. In Arkansas, females as small as $5^7/8$ inches (15.0 cm) snout-vent length have developed follicles indicating sexual maturity. These individuals presumably could produce offspring at the age of 2 years (Trauth, 1984).

General information: Known predators of this lizard include the white-tailed hawk *Buteo albicaudatus* (Stevenson, 1946) and the prairie kingsnake *Lampropeltis calligaster* (McConkey, 1954). Glass lizard tracks can easily be differentiated from snake tracks. They leave a wildly undulating track in smooth sand that shows that they have poor traction. The track leaves the impression that the lizard was trying to burrow through the sandy ridges rather than go over them as most snakes would.

Snapping Turtles
(Family — Chelydridae)

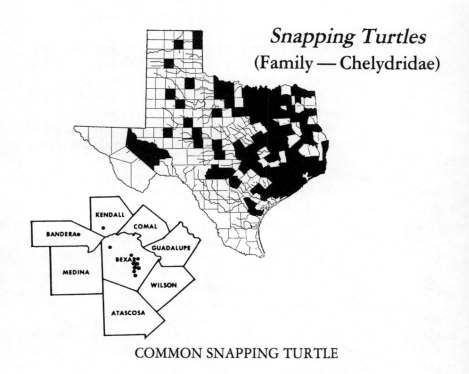

COMMON SNAPPING TURTLE

Chelydra serpentina serpentina (Linnaeus) 1758

Members of this family range from southern Canada to northwestern South America and include some of the largest freshwater turtles in the world. *Chelydra s. serpentina* ranges from southern Canada, south to the Gulf of Mexico and west to the Rocky Mountains, with other subspecies in southern Florida and tropical America. This turtle, well-deserving of its vernacular name, is noted for its long neck and tail, and short temper. Adults usually average 10 to 35 pounds (4.5 to 13.6 kg). One large, purposefully overfed, captive specimen was reported by Pope (1946) to weigh 86 pounds (39 kg). Ernst and Barbour (1972) reported a wild-caught Kentucky turtle weighing 75 pounds (34 kg).

Identification: Adults of this large aquatic species have a carapace that varies from olive-brown to dark brown, with juveniles tending to be a dark

90

brown to almost gray-black. Juveniles usually have a pattern of radiating lines on each enlarged dorsal scale or scute, frequently with white spots at the edge of the upper and lower marginals; the plastron is black or brown with some light mottling. The relatively small plastron of adults is an unpatterned yellowish to tan (occasionally reddish). Skin color is grayish-black with whitish or yellow spots. A faint light area is often behind the eye; jaws are marked with horizontal dark streaks.

Other characteristics include a *rough, broad, oval carapace with 3 moderately well-defined, serrated, longitudinal ridges on the young;* ridges reduced or absent in older specimens, except for the areolan tubercle on the vertebral and costal region; 22 marginal scales around the rim of carapace; nuchal scute wider than long; large, stout head with very powerful, hook-like jaws, and short snout; two barbels on chin, with numerous, small, wart-like tubercles on legs and neck; eyes visible if viewed from above; long, thick claws on webbed feet; *long tail equaling or exceeding the carapace in length, and armored on top with 3 saw-toothed rows of tubercles, the median row having the larger tubercles.*

There are no other long-tailed species in the region.

Size: The common snapping turtle in South Central Texas frequently exceeds 10 to 12 inches (25.4 to 30.5 cm) in carapace length. Gerholdt and Oldfield (1987) reported the record length for the species at $19^{3}/_{8}$ inches (49.4 cm). The author found a carapace at South Side Lions Park Lake in southern San Antonio that measured 14 inches (35.6 cm) in length.

Behavior: This large, aquatic turtle usually stalks its prey in slow-motion, suddenly lunging out with incredible speed to grab its food. Snapping turtles seldom leave the water except to lay their eggs, and while they are usually not aggressive toward humans while underwater, they become extremely pugnacious when moved onto dry land. Moreover, an adult can inflict a rather painful, bloody bite that may require medical attention. The "proper" method of handling this turtle is by holding its long tail; however, care should be taken not to injure a heavy specimen, nor to carelessly let it bite the handler's leg or hand.

Each spring and summer from 1960 through 1968, the author collected several snapping turtles along the San Antonio River above the Espada Dam south of San Antonio. They were often spotted in the warm, muddy shallows with only their nostrils and eyes exposed from the deep mud in which they were buried. When observed during the day, they appeared sluggish until confronted, at which time the turtles rapidly swam to safety. They apparently emerge in late March. Hutchison et al. (1966) found the mean critical thermal maximum of this species was 37.4 to 40.6 C. (99 to 105 F.). These turtles have a high tolerance to low temperatures, are primarily nocturnal in the wild, and tend to be caught frequently on hook and line by fishermen.

Food: The diet of these omnivores includes freshwater snails, crayfish, molluscs and other small aquatic invertebrates, fish, carrion, frogs, toads, reptiles including water snakes (*Nerodia*), small mammals, waterfowl, and aquatic plants.

Habitat: Chelydra serpentina can be found in almost any permanent body of water that normally supports a community of aquatic plants, but it tends to prefer areas with muddy bottoms and banks in which it can bury itself. Reported habitats include rivers, streams, ponds, lakes, swamps, and even brackish marshes along the coast. It is not commonly found in fast-flowing streams, except where deep, silt-filled pools have formed by impoundment (damming) of the stream. Turtles in clear water tend to stay hidden under debris in deeper water during the day.

Breeding: White and Murphy (1973) observed in a Tennessee population that the spermatogenic cycle is at its peak from July to September. The author has observed two large females laying eggs, one in late May and another in early June at South Side Lions Park Lake in San Antonio. These turtles excavated the nest by digging a hole with alternating actions of their hind feet. The nest was about 5 to 7 inches (12.7 to 17.8 cm) and 3 inches (7.6 cm) across the entrance, increasing in dimension toward the bottom of the hole. The nest was located in dark-colored clay soil about 3 to 4 yards (3.2 to 4.3 m) from the nearest water. One nest site was well-drained and the other was in an area that floods during heavy rains. Both turtles deposited one egg about every minute. Egg-laying can occur from late May through June (Iverson, pers. comm.). Pritchard (1979) reported that this turtle lays an average of 25 eggs per clutch, although 50 to 60 eggs are reported from Great Plains populations (Iverson, pers. comm.). The white, spherical, flexible eggs are laid in one clutch and measure 1⅛ inches (29 mm) in diameter. Depending on the weather, the time to hatching in South Central Texas is usually 11 to 13 weeks. Hatchlings are approximately 1 to 1⅛ inches (25 to 29 mm) in carapace length, and almost as wide.

92

Males may be distinguished by the position of the vent, which is located more posteriorly on the tail. Also, males generally tend to have a shorter plastron and narrower bridge. Females apparently can retain viable sperm for several years. Ernst and Barbour (1972) reported that both sexes become sexually mature when the carapace is about 8 inches (20.3 cm) long, while White and Murphy (1973) reported that both sexes become sexually mature at about 5³/₄ inches (14.6 cm) plastron length.

General information: The common snapping turtle usually has abundant, greenish algae growing on its carapace. This may provide some degree of camouflage, or may simply be a passive consequence of its highly aquatic life. Occasionally, adults are caught in substantial numbers by fishermen for making stew or soup. The maximum longevity for this species in captivity, as reported by the Philadelphia Zoo, is 38 years.

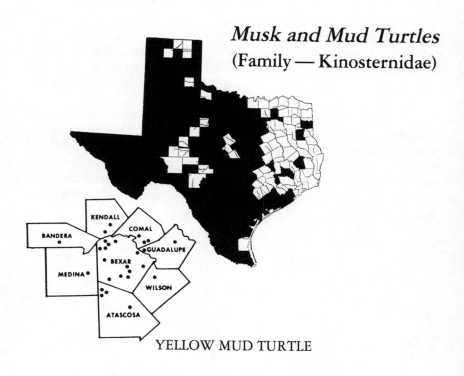

Musk and Mud Turtles
(Family — Kinosternidae)

YELLOW MUD TURTLE

Kinosternon flavescens flavescens (Agassiz) 1857

The yellow mud turtle is a member of the New World family Kinosternidae, which is represented by 4 genera and approximately 25 species, 16 of which occur in the genus *Kinosternon*. *Kinosternon f. flavescens* ranges from northern Nebraska to eastern Mexico, and as far west as Arizona, with isolated populations in extreme southeastern Kansas and adjacent Missouri. A second subspecies occurs in southern Arizona and northern Mexico. This species is a common inhabitant throughout much of South Central Texas.

When disturbed, the yellow mud turtle expels a strong, musky secretion from paired glandular openings on each side of the bridge.

Identification: This species has a carapace that is essentially a uniform dull yellowish or olive-green to olive-brown, with hatchlings having a light spot at the posterior borders of the marginal scutes on the carapace. The bridge, the

94

underside of the marginals, and the plastron have yellowish with dark pigment along the seams, although the plastron may be occasionally brown instead of yellow. The chin and throat may be variably white or yellowish; the upper head is olive-gray; and the remainder of the skin is uniform gray.

Other identifying characters include *ninth and tenth marginal scutes of adults and large juveniles are distinctly higher than the eighth marginal, and the ninth marginal is peaked upward where it meets the seam area between the costal scutes.* Small juveniles, up to 2¹/₂ inches (6.4 cm) long, and hatchlings have the ninth and tenth marginals at approximately the same height as the eighth. However, the ninth is always distinctly peaked toward the top, rising only slightly above the upper edge of the eighth and tenth marginal.

Kinosternon f. flavescens has a relatively flat, smooth, and oval carapace with 23 marginal scutes (including the nuchal). The marginals are slightly wider than they are high (marginals 1 through 8 only). The wide, slightly concave plastron is notched at the rear. The plastron is not large enough to allow an individual to completely close the shell, although two well-developed transverse hinges enable closure of each end independently. Males differ from females in having a relatively smaller and occasionally concave plastron, a long, thick tail with a horny spur at the tip, and rough scale patches on the inside of the hind limbs. Both sexes have small barbels on the underside of the neck, and slightly larger ones on the chin.

Similar species in the area include the Mississippi mud turtle (*Kinosternon subrubrum hippocrepis*), which is distinguished by having the ninth marginal scute approximately the same height as or only slightly higher than the eighth, and by the presence of two light head stripes. The common musk turtle (*Sternotherus odoratus*) has two light stripes on the head and a small, single-hinged plastron.

Size: The average carapace length of the yellow mud turtle is approximately 4 to 5 inches (10.2 to 12.7 cm), with the record length being 6³/₈ inches (16.2 cm).

Behavior: Mahmoud (1969) reports that in an Oklahoma population the optimum body temperature is approximately 25.06 C. (78 F.) and the maximum temperature tolerance is 43.25 C. (110 F.). Mud turtles are normally timid and very seldom attempt to bite, but they may expel a strong, musky secretion if disturbed. During rainy weather they may be found on roads at considerable distances from water.

The mud turtle is active during the day and is often observed during the midday foraging in shallow mud flats. According to Iverson (pers. comm.), *K. flavescens* forages in primarily aquatic habitat, although it is rarely observed terrestrially. In South Central Texas, terrestrial foraging has occasionally been observed during early morning and evening hours.

Studies in Iowa, Oklahoma, and New Mexico indicate that the earliest activity following hibernation is in April, while the first feeding takes place in May (Mahmoud, 1969; Christiansen and Dunham, 1972). Mud turtles tend to remain in shallow water until temperatures increase in spring. Much basking has been reported during this period. Comparisons by Christianson et al. (1985) show that the timing of both April movement and May feeding activities in New Mexico and Iowa populations coincide at about the same time. Aestivation in South Central Texas and New Mexico also starts at approximately the same time (mid-August through September, pers. obser.). The duration of activity, as compiled from 66 South Central Texas observations available to the author, is generally from April through the end of October. Two February records are exceptions. When inactive, during the cooler months or episodic warm spells, these turtles are buried under leaf litter, piles of debris, under the mud in the water, or have taken refuge in various holes in the bank.

Food: This carnivorous turtle is rather opportunistic in its feeding behavior, consuming any prey that can be overpowered. It is also considered a scavenger. The aquatic diet includes flatworms, roundworms, annelids, crustaceans, adult insects and larvae, snails, fish, and larval amphibians. During terrestrial foraging they will take earthworms, centipedes, millipedes, spiders, and insects.

Habitat: This turtle inhabits almost any body of water within its range, including temporary ponds with little aquatic vegetation. Habitats may thus include cattle tanks, ponds in semiarid grasslands or open woodlands, roadside puddles, sewer drains, irrigation ditches, sinkholes, seasonally dry ponds, lakes, reservoirs, slow-moving creeks and rivers, sloughs, and swamps. Kofron and Schreiber (1985) stated that this turtle appears to tolerate major alterations of its natural habitat.

Breeding: Reproduction of this species has not been studied in South Central Texas. However, testes from male turtles from Arkansas, Texas, and Oklahoma indicated that the spermatogenetic cycle starts in June and reaches a peak in mid-August (Mahmoud and Klicka, 1972). The earliest ovulation reported from several adjoining

96

states was in mid-May. Copulation has been observed primarily during the spring, and occasionally in the fall. Female growth of large egg follicles starts after oviposition, and these follicles reach ovulatory size before the following breeding season.

Egg-laying usually starts in late May through early to mid-June, with 1 to 6 eggs (4 to 5 average) laid in 1 (or possibly 2) clutches throughout the season. Present data (Christian and Dunham, 1972; Long, 1986) suggest that this species possibly lays 2 clutches of eggs per year in the South Central Texas area. The elliptical, hard-shelled, white eggs average 1 inch (25 mm) by $5/8$ inch (16 mm). As with many reptiles there appears to be a positive correlation between female body size and clutch size.

Hatchlings have a carapace length of $13/16$ to $1^3/16$ inches (21 to 30 mm) at hatching. Adults are reported to become sexually mature in West Texas at about $3^3/4$ to $3^{15}/16$ inches (9.5 to 10.0 cm) or 8 to 9 years (Long, 1986).

General information: On May 9, 1974, a rice field near Chocolate Bayou, Brazoria County, Texas, was treated with an insecticide called aldrin, which is metabolized rapidly to dieldrin in warm-blooded animals and freshwater fish. This insecticide apparently caused a female yellow mud turtle, found at the site on June 8, 1974, to go into a state of ataxia (swimming on its side in circles). A later laboratory analysis of the dead turtle indicated that it contained 4 ppm aldrin, 47 ppm dieldrin, and was apparently suffering from insecticide poisoning (Flickinger and Mulhern, 1980).

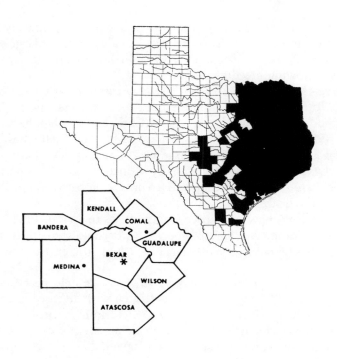

MISSISSIPPI MUD TURTLE

Kinosternon subrubrum hippocrepis Gray 1856

This species of *Kinosternon* occurs over most of the southeastern United States. One of 3 subspecies, the Mississippi mud turtle ranges from southeastern Missouri and the eastern half of Oklahoma, south to the Gulf of Mexico from extreme southwestern Alabama to Central Texas. Although it is still relatively abundant in eastern Texas, this turtle is now extremely rare or possibly absent in South Central Texas. Cope recorded one specimen before 1915 from Medina County, Strecker lists another before 1927, and Olson reported one taken in 1957–58 from Bexar County. Two other preserved specimens from Comal County are in the Los Angeles County Museum and Texas A&I University collections.

Identification: The adult carapace is a relatively uniform olive to brown, the plastron yellowish or brownish. The brown to yellow coloration is sometimes accented by a darker color along the plastral seams. *Moderately distinct, light yellowish stripes are usually found on each side of the head.* One stripe is above and the other usually below the eye at a slight downward angle relative to the jaws. These stripes are normally unbroken. The dark olive or dark gray head of adults may be mottled laterally with light yellowish spots that are often obscurely aligned with the head stripes.

Hatchlings have a dusky brown skin with 2 faint yellow lines on the neck and side of the head. On the underside of each marginal scute there is a round, light orange spot. The plastron has ten paired, irregular, red to orange spots on a black ground color. The reddish color usually fades to yellow as they get older, and is completely lost in 1 or 2 years.

Other identifying characters include *ninth marginal scute on adults and juveniles of approximately the same height as, or only slightly higher than, the eighth;* carapace smooth, oval, and elongated with a weak vertebral keel and 2 weak, blunt, lateral keels on hatchlings; plastron double-hinged with 11 scutes, the anterior plastral part shorter than its posterior counterpart.

Males differ from females in having a longer, relatively thicker tail with a blunt spine at the tip; the vent is located beyond the carapace; a concave plastron that is deeply notched posteriorly; and rough scale patches on the inside of the hind legs. Both sexes have small barbels on the underside of the neck and slightly larger ones on the chin. This aquatic species has webbed feet.

A similar species found in South Central Texas is the yellow mud turtle (*Kinosternon flavescens flavescens*). It is distinguished by the lack of head stripes, and having the ninth and tenth marginal scutes on adults and juveniles (larger than $2^1/2$ inches, 63 mm in length), distinctly higher than the eighth marginal, the ninth marginal peaked where it meets the seam area between the costal scutes. Another similar turtle is the common musk turtle (*Sternotherus odoratus*). It has a highly arched carapace and a small, inconspicuous, single-hinged plastron.

Size: The Mississippi mud turtle is a small turtle, usually reaching only 3 to 4 inches (7.6 to 10.2 cm) in length. Its record carapace length is only $4^7/8$ inches (12.4 cm).

Behavior: This aquatic turtle may be occasionally found during rainy weather migrating on land from one body of water to another. Strecker in 1893 witnessed a mass migration of 45 turtles from a marsh location to a large tank over half a mile away. On other occasions, as an aquatic habitat dries up, they will burrow into the mud to presumably aestivate. These mud turtles are considered to be primarily muddy-bottom dwellers, although they are occasionally observed basking on emergent brush and on the shore.

Mahmoud (1969) reported that males and females in an Oklahoma population have a home range that averages 0.12 acres and 01.13 acres, respectively. He also reported a two-peaked daily activity pattern for this subspecies from June through August, observing that morning activity occurred between 4:00 and 9:00 A.M. with a peak between 5:20 and 8:00 A.M., and that afternoon and evening activity occurred between 4:40 and 10:00 P.M. with the peak activity between 7:00 and 8:00 P.M. Depending on temperature and other conditions, these turtles are reported to be active throughout the year in the southern parts of their range. They usually burrow in the soft mud bottom of a watercourse, beneath logs or piles of debris, or may dig a burrow away from the water source. They usually remain mostly inactive in such situations until March or early April. This subspecies has been reported to have an upper temperature tolerance of 40.95 C. (106 F.). The Mississippi mud turtle is capable of expelling a strong, musky secretion if disturbed. Although most individuals are quite timid, they have been reported to occasionally bite when captured.

Food: Mississippi mud turtles are considered rather opportunistic in their feeding behavior, and, according to one Oklahoma study, they prefer insects, molluscs, and aquatic vegetation (Mahmoud, 1968), but they will also consume amphibian larvae, crustaceans, and carrion.

Habitat: Habitat preferences include slow-moving bodies of shallow water with soft muddy bottoms, quiet sloughs, marshes, ditches with fluctuating water levels and considerable aquatic vegetation, wet meadows, ponds, and cypress swamps. According to Pritchard (1979), this turtle has a high tolerance for saline conditions; it is considered abundant on the inner edges of tidal marshes and offshore islands of Texas.

Breeding: Mahmoud and Klicka (1972) report that the male reproductive cycle, as reflected by gross morphological changes in the testes and sperm ducts, begins in June and reaches a peak in mid-August. Copulation takes place during the spring (Skorepa and Ozment, 1968). Ovulation and oviposition occur from early May through June (April to mid-July in Arkansas; Iverson, 1979). Nesting begins by mid-March in East Texas, based on the presence of eggs in a turtle examined in March (Houseal and Carr, 1983). The female digs a shallow nest, 3 to 5 inches (7.6 to 12.7 cm) deep, at about a 30-degree angle in loose soil or organic debris. The female may excavate at several sites before finding an acceptable one.

Initial digging is done with the front limbs and completed with the hind limbs. In South Central Texas, this turtle probably lays 3 clutches of 2 to 5 eggs per year (Iverson, pers. comm.). However, there are several records throughout the geographic range of only 1 clutch per season (Gibbons et al., 1982). Body size may be independently or interactively important in influencing clutch size in this species (Gibbons, 1983).

The white to pinkish-white, brittle-shelled, elliptical eggs usually measure $7/8$ to $1 1/8$ inches (22 to 29 mm) by $9/16$ to $5/8$ inch (15 to 16 mm). Average incubation time ranges from 90 to 119 days, with hatchlings appearing in August and September. Hatchlings, both male and female, reach sexual maturity at $2 3/4$ to $3 1/8$ inches (7.0 to 8.0 cm) in carapace length throughout the range (Gibbons, 1983). Temperatures during egg development apparently play a part in the sex determination of many turtle species; e.g., with certain species of turtles, previous laboratory studies indicate that only females develop at 88 F. (31 C.) and above.

General information: Pope (1939) reported a captive of this species that lived for 38 years.

The scientific name for this species (*K. subrubrum*) means in Latin: *sub* = under, and *rubrum* = red, in reference to the reddish plastron of hatchlings.

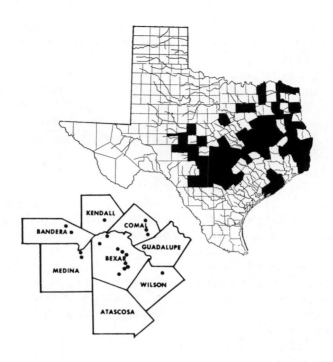

COMMON MUSK TURTLE

Sternotherus odoratus (Latreille) 1801

The musk turtle, *Sternotherus odoratus,* is a small aquatic turtle that is sometimes called the stinkpot turtle. It is a member of the family Kinosternidae and is closely related to mud turtles of the genus *Kinosternon.* Moreover, based on similarities in proteins, shell kinesis and karyotypes, Seidel et al. (1986) concluded that the present generic concepts of *Sternotherus* and *Kinosternon* are questionable and placed *Sternotherus* in the synonymy of *Kinosternon.*

Of the 4 recognized species in the genus *Sternotherus,* the common musk turtle has a wide distribution, ranging from the east coast of Maine and southern Ontario to southern Florida, and west to Wisconsin, Kansas, Oklahoma, into eastern and Central Texas.

Identification: Adults may have an irregularly streaked or unmarked, smooth, dull olive-brown to dark gray carapace, often caked

102

with algae or mud. The plastron of the adult is dull yellow, and the *head and neck are dark olive to black with two prominent or partly obscured light yellow lines on each side.* These two stripes start on the snout, run posteriorly above and below each eye, and onto the neck. The skin is generally dark olive. Juveniles have a dark gray to black carapace which may become paler with age, revealing a spotted pattern. The young also have a small white spot at the edge of each marginal scute, which disappears with age. The mottled, black plastron eventually fades to a dull yellow.

Another identifying character is a highly arched, smooth, oval carapace. The prominent vertebral keel, along with the smaller lateral keels found in juveniles, are eventually lost when sexual maturity is reached. The carapace becomes proportionally lower and more elongate with age. *The plastron is small and has a single hinge.* These turtles have a small gular shield, and barbels on the chin and throat.

Males differ from females in possessing a thicker and longer tail (which terminates as a blunt spur), a shorter plastron, larger areas of soft skin between the plastral scutes, and having rough patches of tilted scales on the inner surface of the rear limbs. Females have only small areas of skin showing between the plastral scutes, and a very small tail. Both sexes have webbed feet.

Similar species include the yellow mud turtle (*Kinosternon flavescens flavescens*), which is distinguished by a much larger plastron with two hinges, and by not having two light head stripes, and the Mississippi mud turtle (*Kinosternon subrubrum hippocrepis*), which additionally has a large plastron with two hinges.

Size: The common musk turtle is one of the smallest turtles in South Central Texas. Whereas it is not unusual to find mature 3- to 4-inch (7.6 to 10.2 cm) individuals in the streams and rivers of the region, the record carapace length is 5³/₈ inches (13.7 cm).

Behavior: This highly aquatic species is primarily nocturnal, although it has been observed by the author in the early morning at his Espada Dam study area on the San Antonio River. Here these turtles were usually first seen at dawn and thereafter to about 10:00 A.M., from early May through early September. In late September through early December, and March through April, as water temperatures dipped below 65 F. (18.5 C.), activity tended to be restricted to midday and early afternoon. Turtles are apparently inactive when the water temperature drops below 55 F. (12.5 C.). Whereas Legler (1943), Carr (1952), Ernst and Barbour (1972), and others have reported nocturnal

103

activity in this species, Jon Lowell and the author have made over 300 nocturnal observations at Espada Dam over three years without once seeing a night-active individual.

In contrast to the mud turtles, the musk turtle is rarely found away from water, even after a heavy rain. Occasionally, the author has observed individuals emerging from the water to bask on the bank or on logs with other species. The musk turtle appears to prefer exposing the upper portion of its carapace to the sunlight as it rests in shallow water, or when resting among aquatic vegetation. Jon Lowell observed one on a branch over 6 feet (1.8 m) above the water at Salado Creek in Fort Sam Houston. According to Mahmoud (1969), the common musk turtle prefers to maintain a body temperature of about 75 F. (24.1 C.) in its natural habitat.

Food: This turtle feeds mainly on small molluscs, carrion, a variety of invertebrates (insects, crayfish), fish, and aquatic vegetation.

Habitat: The bottom-dwelling musk turtle is found in a broad variety of permanent watercourses of varying depths, with little or no current and a soft muddy bottom. Such habitats include rivers, streams, clear watercourses, ponds, lakes, sloughs, swamps, and canals. According to Conant (1936), it is not tolerant of brackish water.

Breeding: In the southern United States, male and female common musk turtles mature in about 3 years (Tinkle, 1961). Average size at maturity for male *S. odoratus* is about 2⁹/₁₆ inches (6.5 cm) carapace length, and 3¹/₄ inches (8.3 cm) for females (Ibid.). Mating has been observed in April and May, and in September and October. According to Ernst and Barbour (1972), there is evidence that sperm from late matings may be retained through the winter in the oviducts. They also state that mating occurs underwater, in the shallows, and in the early morning or at night. The egg-laying season (according to limited data) extends from April through July in South Central Texas. It is possible that a common musk turtle from South Central Texas could ovulate at least twice during a single season, although it appears that multiple ovulation in the northern part of its range is unlikely.

Nesting usually takes place from early morning into the late afternoon. The female often seeks areas covered with leaf litter, rotting wood, or soft soil to deposit the eggs in a shallow nest. These turtles usually dig their nest with their hind feet and have been known to share nesting sites. A total of 16 nests were once found under a 3-foot (.91 m) long log, with nests sometimes being interconnected (Cagle, 1937). The eggs usually number 2 to 3 in southern populations, with the average estimated at 3 per clutch in Oklahoma and Arkansas (Fitch, 1985). According to Tinkle (1961), there is a correlation between clutch size and body size, as is true of most turtles. The brittle-shelled, elliptical, white eggs usually measure 1⅛ inches (29 mm) by ⁹/₁₆ inch (15 mm) and do not increase in size during incubation. Incubation under laboratory conditions lasts from 60 to 75 days. Wild hatchlings usually emerge in late summer in South Central Texas and have a carapace length of ¾ to ¹⁵/₁₆ inch (20 to 25 mm).

General information: According to Conant and Hudson (1949), a common musk turtle at the Philadelphia Zoo lived for more than 53 years and 3 months.

The musk turtle lives up to its specific name *odoratus*; *odor* in Latin means "a smell," and *atus* is a suffix meaning "provided with." When handled, this turtle will not hesitate to bite and expel the contents of the musk glands. This foul-smelling, volatile, yellowish fluid is secreted by a pair of glands located on each side of the bridge just below the rim of the carapace.

Map, Cooter, Slider, and Box Turtles

(Family — Emydidae)

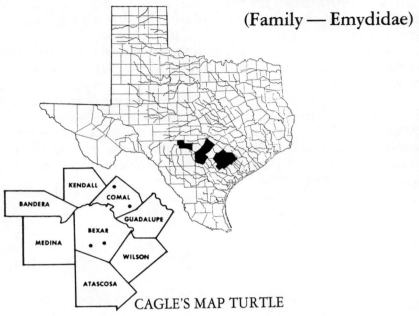

CAGLE'S MAP TURTLE

Graptemys caglei Haynes and McKown 1974

The Cagle's map turtle, *Graptemys caglei,* is a member of the family Emydidae, which includes map, cooter, slider, and box turtles. The family Emydidae is the largest family of living turtles, represented by over 80 species of turtles in tropical and temperate regions of the Northern Hemisphere. There are approximately ten species of *Graptemys* in the eastern U.S., often called "sawbacks" because of the projecting, dorsal keel on the carapace. Several of these species, including *Graptemys caglei,* are endemic to single river drainage systems of the Gulf of Mexico.

Identification: The carapace of this small, aquatic turtle is usually light green and has one or more roughly circular, cream-colored lines on the costal and marginal scutes, with alternating, thinner, irregular, black circles. The vertebral spines on Cagle's map turtles are usually tipped with brown or black, except in most mature females. The plastron is a pale cream with pale black markings extending along the scute seams, and adult males often have black flecks on their plastron. Skin color of the head, neck, and limbs is cream, with a series of black lines forming V-shaped markings on top of the head and curving down behind each eye to form a crescent or J-shaped marking (in 88 percent of those turtles checked; Smith and Brodie, 1982). *There is a wide, cream-colored, transverse band on the lower jaw,* and the limbs have both broad and narrow, well-defined, black and cream-colored stripes extending along them.

Other characteristics include a carapace that is moderately flat, elliptical in adults, with the central portions of the scutes raised above their borders; *knobby, middorsal vertebral keels sharply serrated in juveniles and males* (vertebral keels usually missing or reduced in large adult females). Males of this species have longer claws on their front feet than do females.

One similar species in South Central Texas is the Texas river cooter (*Pseudemys texana*), which is distinguished from the map turtle by having tinges of red around the edge and dark seams on the plastron; the second costal usually has a light vertical or inverted Y-shaped mark on it; no distinct, middorsal, knobby keels occur on the adult carapace; and by the absence of a cream-colored transverse band on the lower jaw. Juvenile Texas river cooters are distinguished by the absence of the jaw marking, and by distinct, dark, thin, curving or encircling lines on each of the marginals.

Size: Male Cagle's map turtles measure from $2^3/4$ to $4^1/2$ inches (7.0 to 11.5 cm) in carapace length. Females are larger, with a carapace length of approximately $6^3/8$ inches (16.2 cm).

Behavior: This turtle is extremely quick to slide from its basking site on logs to the safety of the water. It is thus rarely seen basking, or on land, except when laying eggs. Haynes (pers. comm.) has observed their basking behavior and reports finding them on exposed rocks in shallow waters and on logs and cypress knees in pools and impoundments along the Guadalupe River. The absence of sandbars on this river may cause the nesting habits to differ from those of other species of *Graptemys.* Nevertheless, in certain parts of the Guadalupe River, *Graptemys caglei* may be the dominant aquatic turtle species.

Food: A study of the July stomach contents of map turtles examined by Haynes and McKown (1974) from the Guadalupe River indicated that the diet consisted of both plant and animal matter. However, because the plant matter consisted of twigs, algae, and grass, it was presumed that most of this was ingested incidentally while feeding on insects and other invertebrates.

The juveniles are reported to feed primarily on insects, such as caddis fly larvae, and thin-shelled gastropods. It is possible that different dietary items are utilized during different seasons of the year.

Habitat: The habitat for this predominantly aquatic species includes slow-moving stretches and pools of impounded water, 3 to 10 feet (1 to 3 m) deep, behind small dams in the Guadalupe River system. This map turtle has been found near the headwaters of the Guadalupe River, but there are few records from the river as it flows southeastward across the Edwards Plateau. A few miles northwest of Cuero, on the Guadalupe River in DeWitt County, this species is commonly found basking on fallen trees out in the water, cypress knees, and brush above some of the deeper holes. Although records of this turtle are confirmed from Bexar and Comal counties, it is likely that the species also exists in Kendall and Guadalupe counties. This species has also been found on the Blanco and San Marcos rivers. Haynes (pers. comm.) observed one over 30 years ago in the San Antonio River near the Mission Road Bridge. Although a Cagle's map turtle was possibly collected on the Medina River in southern Bexar County less than 10 years ago, *Graptemys caglei* may now be extirpated in the entire San Antonio River system.

Breeding: Limited information is available on the reproduction of this species. Hatchling turtles have been collected and observed from September through November, which could indicate a late spring to early summer nesting season. Females deposit their eggs in a 6-inch (15.3 cm) deep cavity near the water. The eggs are oval, measuring about 1½ inches (38 mm) in length, and they may be deposited in 2 or 3 clutches each season (Garrett and Barker, 1987). The sex of hatchling map turtles is influenced by incubation temperature of eggs (Bull and Vogt, 1979). According to Bertl (1983), sexual maturity is attained at a carapace length of 2⅜ inches (6.0 cm).

General information: This species was described in 1974 by David Haynes and Ronald McKown and was named after the late Dr. Fred R. Cagle of Tulane University, a well-known authority on turtles.

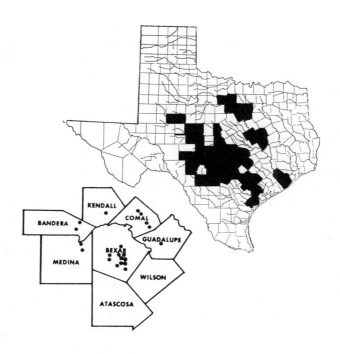

TEXAS RIVER COOTER

Pseudemys texana Baur 1893

In the family Emydidae, the "cooters and sliders" refer to a group of aquatic turtles that have appeared in the literature under three generic names: *Chrysemys, Pseudemys,* and *Trachemys.* The placement of individual species into these genera (and thus which genera should be used) varies among different turtle taxonomists; the scientific names used here for the two South Central Texas forms are *Pseudemys texana* and *Trachemys scripta,* following Ward (1984).

The Texas river cooter, *Pseudemys texana,* is a Texas endemic restricted to the Colorado, Brazos, and Guadalupe/San Antonio River drainages. Within its geographic distribution, however, it may be very abundant; these turtles are so common along the San Antonio River it is not unusual to observe 50 or more basking on logs over a short stretch of appropriate habitat.

In addition to the question of the generic placement of *Pseudemys texana,* there is also taxonomic controversy as to its species status. Some authors consider this form a subspecies of *P. concinna,* a similar turtle found in the river drainages both to the east and west of those inhabited by *P. texana.*

Identification: The carapace appears to be a dark greenish color, primarily due to the substantial algal growth usually found on adults. However, the true color of the *carapace is usually a dark olive-brown with cream or yellowish markings, occasionally tinged with light orange on the yellow markings.* There are thin, curving, yellowish lines on the carapace that create whorls or concentric circles. Individuals may have a light vertical bar at the center of each marginal scute. *The underside of the marginal scutes are usually marked with dark concentric lines which create whorls bordering the seams.* The plastron is yellow and may be tinged with reddish-orange at the dark seams, especially toward the anterior half of the plastron. The dark color of the plastron is often lost along the seams in adults. Juveniles have distinct markings and patterns, but older adult males and some females lose pattern with age. Furthermore, markings may be totally absent in extremely old adults.

The *distinct yellow head markings are variable* and may include several spots and stripes which are either joined together or separated by dark color. These markings may include a Y-shaped yellow mark, yellow chin stripe, and bars which often extend vertically just behind and below the eye. There are also other yellow head markings that curve upward and around the Y-shaped or bar-like markings. The skin is dark olive to brown, with several thin, light yellow, or orange-tinged stripes on the limbs. The carapace is elongated and narrow, moderately flat, and curves evenly up to the highest point of the vertebral scutes. These scutes may be slightly serrated posteriorly, especially in juveniles. The broad upper jaw is notched and cusped on each side; the lower jaw is serrated and terminates in a tooth-like projection flanked by cusp-like projections on both sides. The plastron is hingeless. Males have long, straight foreclaws (used during courtship), a thick tail, and an anal opening behind the posterior carapacial marginals. The feet in both sexes are webbed.

Another similar species in South Central Texas is Cagle's map turtle (*Graptemys caglei*), which is distinguished by a wide, cream-colored, transverse band on the lower jaw, and sharply serrated, knobby, middorsal, vertebral keels on juveniles and males.

Size: In South Central Texas, adult females average from 6 to 10

110

inches (15.2 to 25.4 cm) in length, and adult males are slightly smaller. Additionally, the author has measured a 13-inch (33 cm) long female that was collected from the San Antonio River.

Behavior: These turtles adapt well to habitat modification and channelization of rivers, provided adequate basking sites and some aquatic vegetation are available. The temperature tolerance of this species must be rather high since it may bask for hours on logs on moderately warm days without plunging into the water. Moreover, it occasionally shares basking sites with other species of turtles. *Pseudemys texana* has been observed foraging on river bottoms, or resting on the bottom, and periodically coming to the surface to breathe. It seldom ventures overland unless nesting.

Food: Strecker (1927) found molluscs in the digestive tract of these turtles. Young specimens actively pursue aquatic and terrestrial insects, crayfish, snails, and other invertebrates when offered. Adults are expected to also feed on aquatic vegetation and carrion, as do the cooters of the Southeast. Such increased consumption of plant material is a dietary shift that occurs in most emydid turtles as they become adults (Hart, 1983). Because of these turtles' scavenging habits, many fishermen consider them to be a nuisance. Nevertheless, because they play an important part in the aquatic food web, *Pseudemys texana* should be viewed with greater tolerance.

Habitat: This turtle is the most common species observed in South Central Texas. It occurs in most watercourses of Bexar, Medina, Bandera, Kendall, Comal, and Guadalupe counties, and is likely also to be found in Wilson County and possibly Atascosa County. This species is extremely common in the channelized, impounded, or other deepwater areas of Salado and Leon creeks, and along the San Antonio River. It appears to prefer slow-moving water with abundant aquatic vegetation, and also is commonly found in area ponds, lakes, or creeks, and occasionally in cattle tanks or large drainage ditches.

Breeding: Little is known concerning its reproductive habits. They are reported by different sources to lay 4 to 19 eggs. The author and his students saw 3 females digging nests in shallow, 4- to 5-inch (10.2 to 12.7 cm) deep holes in clay soil about 10 to 12 feet (3 to 3.6 m) from the water's edge. Two of the females left for the water after they spotted the observers, thus not completing the egg-laying process, and the third female completed the nest but never laid eggs. Eggs obtained from another source were fine, granular-textured, and dull, measuring about 1³/₈ inches (35 mm) in length. Nesting probably oc-

111

curs in late May and June, and it is suspected that eggs may also be deposited in July. In South Central Texas, hatchlings appear in August and September. Males are reported to mature in three years and females in six or more years (Garrett and Barker, 1987).

Pseudemys previously studied for temperature-dependent sex determination have shown a positive response (Bull et al., 1982); i.e., in all experiments with emydid turtles the hatchlings from warm temperatures are entirely or mostly females, while the hatchlings from cool temperatures are entirely male (Bull and Vogt, 1979).

General information: Normal predators for this turtle's eggs include skunks, raccoons, and opossums. Pollution of the San Antonio River apparently has not forced this turtle into decline. It appears to be much more common today than it was 25 years ago at the old Espada Dam and Brackenridge Park areas on the San Antonio River.

The type locality for *Pseudemys texana* is San Antonio, Texas.

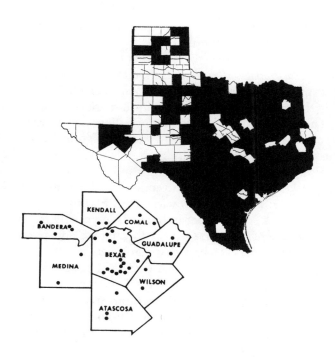

RED-EARED SLIDER

Trachemys scripta elegans (Wied) 1838

Trachemys scripta is primarily an aquatic turtle that ranges from eastern New Mexico to Indiana, and south through the Mississippi River Valley to the southeastern states. The form occurring over most of Texas is *T. s. elegans,* the red-eared slider.

Those who lived in San Antonio and had an interest in turtles during the 1960s remember how rare Texas river cooters, *Pseudemys texana,* were in the San Antonio River, and how abundant were the red-eared sliders. Today, although some lakes and other streams in the area have large red-eared slider populations, Texas river cooters currently outnumber this species by a substantial margin over most Bexar County sections of the San Antonio River. The cause of this dramatic reversal in abundance is unknown, but may be the result of competition between the two species or to changes in environmental factors (e.g., different pollution regimes).

Identification: Trachemys scripta elegans can usually be identified by the *broad, reddish stripe or blotch just behind the eye,* although some adults do not display this color. Older males occasionally have this blotch obscured with a grayish color, or the reddish mark may be otherwise reduced. The head is greenish with narrow yellow stripes, and the skin is green to olive-brown with yellow stripes. Young turtles have a brightly colored carapace, usually dark green with variable light yellow streaking on costal shields and light and dark stripes, bars, circles, and whorl-like markings (older juveniles are sometimes covered with algae). The plastron is yellowish with large, blackish smudge spots in the middle of each scute. Older individuals, especially males, may develop dark pigment, appearing on both carapace and plastron in the form of blotches, spots, or bars that run together, almost completely obscuring the details of the original pattern. On occasion, melanistic individuals are found in the South Central Texas area.

Also characteristic is the oval, medium-sized carapace, convex at the sides and relatively flat above (slightly higher and weakly keeled on younger specimens), and slightly serrated on the posterior margin. This species has an *upper and lower jaw that is rounded along the cutting edge;* sexually mature males have long foreclaws: and the plastron is hingeless.

Similar species in South Central Texas include the Texas river cooter (*Pseudemys texana*) and Cagle's map turtle (*Graptemys caglei*), neither of which have the broad, reddish stripe or blotch just behind the eye, or the numerous dark markings on the plastron.

Size: Adult females collected by the author in South Central Texas range from about 6 to 11 inches (15.2 to 28.0 cm) in carapace length, with the largest female found being 11³/₈ inches (28.9 cm). Males are generally smaller than females, with the largest male seen at 9⁵/₈ inches (24.5 cm).

Behavior: Basking sites for these turtles include stumps, logs, brush, flat rocks, and occasionally water hyacinths and other projections above the water. Such sites are located in a quiet area away from the bank, or on the bank in difficult to approach, heavily vegetated areas. These turtles are occasionally seen basking side by side with the Texas river cooter, *Pseudemys texana.* Because of the relatively mild winters in South Central Texas, these turtles may bask on sunny midafternoon days during January and February. When water temperatures drop below 50 F. (10 C.), however, they do not emerge.

Food: The diet of this species apparently changes with age (Clark and Gibbons, 1969; Hart, 1983). Juveniles are predominantly carnivorous, feeding on aquatic and other adult and larval insects, crayfish, shrimp, amphipods, snails and other molluscs, tadpoles, and small fish. The author feeds his captive juvenile sliders fresh crayfish, insects, fish, raw beef, chicken hearts, and dog food mixed with some vegetables. They tend to leave the vegetables unless they are disguised in the meat. As wild adults become older, however, they tend to progressively eat more aquatic vegetable matter (Hart, 1983). Nevertheless, in captivity these turtles eat almost any food item offered.

Webb (1961) theorized that this turtle's omnivorous habits allow it to thrive in places where fluctuating water levels alternate the availability of different foods, a condition often seen in South Central Texas ponds.

Habitat: This subspecies is found in a wide variety of habitats, including almost all slow-moving rivers and streams in South Central Texas, most ponds, in some cattle tanks, and many of the lakes. They make frequent overland journeys between bodies of water, and during the spring and summer it is not unusual in Wilson or Atascosa counties to see these turtles on the highway as they move from one pond to another. Although this turtle prefers bodies of water with soft muddy bottoms throughout most of South Central Texas, it is occasionally found on the Edwards Plateau in rocky streams with substantial aquatic vegetation.

Breeding: In the Panhandle of Texas, the spermatogenic cycle is under way by mid-May, and the activity peaks during August through September (Brewer and Killebrew, 1986). The red-eared slider has been observed mating in South Central Texas during the spring, with nesting occurring in late May, June, and July. The flexible, $1^3/8$- to $1^1/2$-inch (35 to 38 mm) long, white-shelled eggs increase in size and become more rigid as water is absorbed during incubation. Generally, this species lays 4 to 12 eggs per clutch (more eggs have been reported), with Webb (1961) reporting 3 clutches per season in Oklahoma (mean of 8.8 eggs per clutch). It is probable that females in South Central Texas deposit more than 1 clutch per season, with the monthly timing varying individually and from year to year (Gibbons et al., 1982).

This is another turtle that the author has observed nesting. The female digs a nest cavity with its hind feet to a depth of about 4 or more inches (10.2 cm). As was the case of *Pseudemys texana,* the hind feet were used to enlarge the bottom of the slightly slanting cavity (turtles always empty their cloacal bladder to moisten and soften the soil for easy digging in the clay soil). This individual was apparently not satisfied with the site, which was about 13 feet (3.9 m) from the water's edge, and it returned to the water without laying any eggs. Apparently, this behavior is a fairly common practice with *Trachemys* and *Pseudemys* in South Central Texas; however, the presence of a human, 40 feet (12.1 m) away, may have contributed to her hesitation and ultimate rejection of the site. The incubation period varies from 60 to 75 days, and the hatchlings emerge in July through early September. Hatchlings usually have a carapace length of 1¹/₄ to 1¹/₂ inches (32 to 38 mm) in length. Males mature at an earlier age and smaller size than females. Females become mature in about 6 to 10 years, or 6 to 7¹/₂ inches (15.2 to 19.0 cm) in carapace length. The temperature of the water, as well as food quality, affect growth rates and reproductive potential in this species (Gibbons et al., 1979; Parmenter, 1980).

General information: Predators in South Central Texas include alligators and raccoons, but people are mostly responsible for the killing of these turtles. Over the years, the author has observed several basking turtles shot with pellet guns and .22-caliber rifles. Additionally, fishermen often behead these turtles, rather than remove the hooks from their mouths, and many are crushed on highways by motor vehicles.

Young red-eared sliders were sold in great numbers through the pet industry in the 1950s and 1960s. In the early 1970s, however, a substantial number of human salmonella (bacterial) infections were traced to the pet turtle trade. The red-eared slider was soon thereafter considered one of the principal vectors for salmonella, and warnings were issued by conservationists and biologists concerning the potential contamination of food by captives. The baby turtle pet trade collapsed as legislation prohibited further sales, thus easing commercial pressure on natural turtle populations. Aquatic turtles may still be kept without danger of such infections, however, provided the hands are washed thoroughly after touching a pet turtle or the water in which it lives, the container is cleaned regularly, and the water is changed frequently.

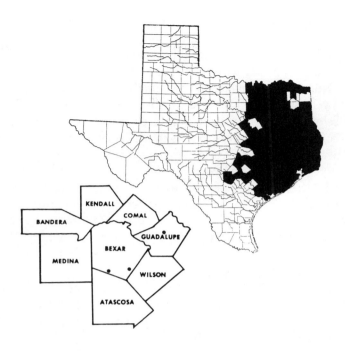

THREE-TOED BOX TURTLE

Terrapene carolina triunguis (Agassiz) 1857

Box turtles of the genus *Terrapene* are terrestrial turtles with a hinged plastron that allows them to completely close the carapace and plastron together at such times when danger threatens. The three-toed box turtle is not uncommon in the eastern half of Texas, but is rare in South Central Texas. It reaches the westernmost limit of its range in the Carrizo Sand Formation of Guadalupe, Wilson, and southern Bexar counties. This subspecies ranges eastward to Missouri and Alabama, with other subspecies elsewhere in the eastern United States. Sometimes individuals have four toes on the hind foot, instead of the three for which the form is named.

Identification: The carapace is dull tan or olive with dark flecks, forming a variable and sometimes obscured pattern. The pattern, if present, may consist of tan lines or spots radiating from the dark area of the upper back section on each carapace scute. The plastron often is butterscotch or creamy yellow and lacks dark spots: some individuals, however, may exhibit dark areas or margins around the scutes. Skin color is usually a brownish-olive to black, with the head, neck, and forelimbs appearing reddish. Numerous, variable, multicolored flecks and dots of orange, white, or yellow occasionally cover the head and front limbs. The dorsal surface of the head is usually a light chocolate-brown. Males have reddish-colored eyes, whereas the iris in the female is usually yellow.

Other distinguishing features include hind feet with *three toes* (exceptionally, four); oval carapace normally tall, rounded, and dome-like; third vertebral scute of the carapace slightly elevated; carapace edges curving slightly upward at the posterior and anterior margins; plastron transversely hinged toward the middle (allowing the shell to close completely). This turtle's upper jaw terminates in a slightly down-curved, beak-like projection. Males occasionally have a concavity on the plastral hind lobe.

The only similar species in the region is the ornate box turtle (*Terrapene ornata ornata*), which is distinguished by having a flattened carapace with a consistent pattern of radiating yellow lines, and on the plastron each scute is similarly patterned.

Size: Three-toed box turtle adults range from 4½ to 5½ inches (11.5 to 14.0 cm) in carapace length, with a record length of 6½ inches (16.5 cm) reported.

Behavior: This species is most active in the early morning hours or after rain showers. *Terrapene carolina triunguis* is not only found near streams but occasionally soaks in them during hot summer months. The daily activities of this species in Montgomery County were monitored by Carr and Houseal (1981), starting on March 17 in early spring. Just after emergence from the hibernaculum of twigs, pine needles, and humus soil in the sand of a pine-oak forest, an adult female was observed basking on brush piles in the sun during midday, and at sunset returning to her hibernaculum. Movements to and from the basking sites were noted as the turtle returned every evening, within an hour before sunset, merely pushing the front part of her body into the forest debris, leaving her head and forelimbs extended. Movement at night was not observed.

Food: The natural diet of this turtle has not been well-studied. In captivity, they are omnivorous and devour earthworms, slugs, grasshoppers, crickets and other insects, carrion, canned dog food, or fruits and vegetable matter. Berries and mushrooms are also known to be included in their diet.

Habitat: Terrapene carolina triunguis is an uncommon resident of the region, with only 6 documented sightings recorded. This turtle may occasionally be seen in Guadalupe County near sandy woodlands or wooded hillsides, meadows, and along streams. In the floodplain of the Guadalupe River, they may be found in association with moderately moist substrates. The development of land and removal of woodland cover may create habitat more favorable to the ornate box turtle, *Terrapene ornata,* found in the area, and thus may account for its local rareness.

Breeding: Little information is available on the reproduction of the subspecies. Along the Gulf Coast, *T. carolina* nests from spring to early summer, laying 2 to 8 elliptical-shaped, thin-shelled, white eggs, measuring $1^3/_8$ inches (35 mm) by $7/_8$ inch (23 mm). Females are reported to be capable of storing viable sperm for reproduction for several years after a mating. The eastern box turtle, *Terrapene carolina carolina,* has been reported (Mount, 1975) to lay 2 or 3 clutches per season, and this may also be the case for the three-toed box turtle in South Central Texas.

General information: The three-toed box turtle is a long-lived species. Various documented records for the species indicate that longevity in the wild ranges from over 25 years to possibly 32 years, although zoo captives have lived over 100 years, according to Ernst (pers. comm.). Box turtles are generally long-lived and make acceptable pets for children. As with any other wild animal, captive turtles must receive proper care and/or should be released back into the wild at the same spot where they were collected.

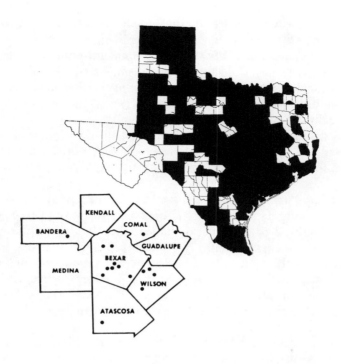

ORNATE BOX TURTLE

Terrapene ornata ornata (Agassiz) 1857

This terrestrial turtle is no longer considered common in South Central Texas. The population dynamics of this species may have been severely affected by the indiscriminate use of DDT (a water-insoluble crystalline insecticide that tends to accumulate in ecosystems and has toxic effects on many vertebrates) in the systematic spraying of crops throughout South Central Texas in the 1950s and 1960s. A few are still found in Wilson, Atascosa, and southern Bexar counties but appear to be in isolated populations.

The ornate box turtle ranges from southern South Dakota and southeastern Wyoming to western Indiana, south to northern Mexico, and through Texas into the coastal prairies of extreme western Louisiana. A second subspecies occurs in far West Texas, New Mexico, and Arizona.

120

Identification: The carapace of this turtle has a dark brown, dark olive, or chocolate ground color. Usually the carapace is marked with a yellow middorsal stripe, and radiating yellow lines are found on each costal scute. The *light yellow lines extend from the 3 yellow spots on each side of the carapace (5 to 9 stripes occur on the second costal scute, and are often broken into rows of light spots).* The plastron has a distinct pattern of yellow lines that radiate across each scute. The skin is olive to dark brown, and yellow spots occur on the dorsal head surface and limbs. The chin and upper jaw are yellowish. As reported for other box turtles, the male usually has a reddish iris, and that of the female is yellow-brown.

Other distinguishing features for adults include carapace round or oval, dorsally flattened; keel along the vertebral scutes on the carapace absent; posterior serrations on the carapace absent; *plastron large, single-hinged,* approximately as long as the carapace. The plastron is hinged slightly anterior to the center. *Four toes* are found on each of the hind feet, with males using the inner hind toe, which is turned inward, for clasping the female shell during mating.

The juvenile carapace is rounded, relatively flatter than the adult, has a rounded yellowish dorsal keel, and is darker than in adults. It also has faint light flecks or spots on the carapace and an indistinct pattern. The light-margined plastron of juveniles has no pattern of light spots on its dark interior area, and the hinge on the plastron is not fully developed in hatchlings.

The only similar species in South Central Texas is the three-toed box turtle (*Terrapene carolina triunguis*), distinguished by its distinctly different pattern on the carapace and plastron, a medial vertebral keel, and (usually) 3 toes on the hind foot.

Size: Average adult carapace length for this turtle is approximately 4 to 5³/₄ inches (10.2 to 14.7 cm). The record carapace length is 6¹/₈ inches (15.6 cm) (Collins, 1982).

Behavior: Published observations indicate that the species is frequently active during warm summer weather in the early mornings (Rose et al., 1988). Usually basking occurs for a short period in the morning before foraging. During the midday hours it occasionally seeks protection from high temperatures in burrows. This species' localized foraging activities may otherwise occur throughout the day when environmental conditions are favorable, particularly on cloudy days, after light rains, during the early morning, or in late afternoon. Ornate box turtles do not enter complete hibernation until the first frost of the year, an event varying substantially in South Central Texas.

Moreover, although these turtles may use animal burrows for temporary shelter, they usually excavate their own hibernacula (Ernst and Barbour, 1972) and may return to the same site in future years (Metcalf and Metcalf, 1979). Emergence from this hibernaculum usually occurs when the soil is sufficiently moist and the air temperature has reached 79 F. (26 C.) (Fitch, 1956). Overall activity in South Central Texas is from March through November.

Food: This opportunistic omnivore's natural diet includes grasshoppers, crickets, caterpillars, flies, beetles and other insects, earthworms, land snails, carrion, fruit, mushrooms, prickly pear, pincushion cactus, and vegetable matter (Legler, 1960; Metcalf and Metcalf, 1970; Blair, 1976; Thomasson, 1980). In captivity they will also accept earthworms, baby mice, dog food, raw beef strips, chicken hearts, and vegetables. Parker (1982) reported opportunistic feeding by this turtle on food items dropped from kite nests that had become concentrated beneath the nest. Metcalf and Metcalf (1970) reported box turtles excavating cow dung for insects, a practice also mentioned by Stebbins (1985).

Habitat: This inhabitant of semiarid plains and open prairie (Parker, 1982) is usually found in the South Central Texas area in sparsely wooded, gently rolling countryside with sandy soil and substantial grass and scattered brush. Other habitats include upland bare grounds, ranges, pastures, fields, and well-drained areas. It is occasionally found near waterways such as Braunig Lake and the nearby riparian woodlands along the San Antonio River as it flows southeastward into Wilson County.

Breeding: This turtle mates throughout the spring, summer, and fall. The male normally pursues the female, nudging the rim of her shell with his head and shell, and later pursues her again from the rear side to mate. Mating may last as long as 30 minutes or more, as the male uses its inner hind toes to hold fast the female's shell. Nesting usually extends from early May through July, but most frequently takes place in June (Ernst, pers. comm.). Moreover, some females may lay a second clutch in July (Ernst and Barbour, 1972). Behler and King (1979) report the female digs a flask-shaped cavity in a well-drained area. Approximately 2 to 8 oval, finely granulated, brittle-shelled white eggs, about 1³/₈ inches (35 mm) long, hatch in 59 to 70 days when incubated at 82 F. (28 C.) to 91 F. (32 C.). As they absorb water, box turtle eggs expand during incubation. Hatchlings have a round carapace about $1^3/16$ to $1^3/8$ inches (30 to 35 mm) long. Adults mature in 7 to 10 years.

General information: Blair (1976) estimated the oldest turtle on a 4.05 hectare (10 acres) study tract in Austin, Texas, was 32 years old, and that a complete turnover of individuals in the population occurred within that 32-year period. Similar findings were reported by Metcalf and Metcalf (1985) on a plot in Kansas. Adults are predated upon by large dogs, coyotes, and badgers, and small turtles are taken by raccoons, skunks, cats, opossums, and hawks. It should be also noted that vehicular traffic causes substantial mortality.

Tortoises
(Family — Testudinidae)

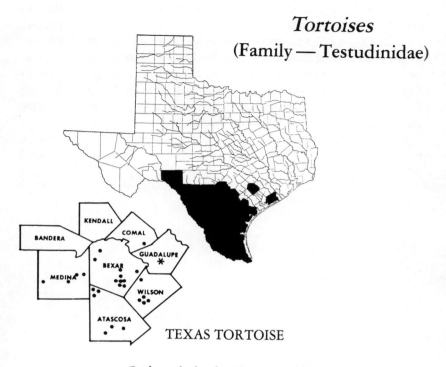

TEXAS TORTOISE

Gopherus berlandieri (Agassiz) 1857

Gopherus berlandieri was named to honor the famous French botanist, Jean Louis Berlandier, one of the earliest (1828 to 1834) writers on Texas amphibians and reptiles. This species is a member of the family Testudinidae, a group represented in most warm temperate and tropical areas of the world, with the exception of Australia. The genus *Gopherus* is represented by four species in North America, but it is the only living genus of tortoise native to the United States. According to some turtle taxonomists, analysis of the qualitative pattern of mitochondrial DNA in gopher tortoises supports the separation of *Gopherus* and *Xerobates* into distinct genera (Bramble, 1971, 1982; Auffenberg, 1976; Lamb, 1989). Such a separation would result in the scientific name of the Texas tortoise becoming *Xerobates berlandieri*.

The Texas tortoise lives in subtropical habitats throughout South

124

Texas and northeastern Mexico, reaching the northernmost limit of its range in Val Verde and Bexar counties. Commercial exploitation by Texas pet dealers and the low reproductive rate of the species was sufficient to motivate the state to protect the Texas tortoise in 1967. Populations today in southern Texas are thought to be stable, but extensive, unfavorable agricultural practices, and the chaining of shrub lands, are eliminating some of their habitats (Rose and Judd, 1982, 1983). In the South Central Texas area this tortoise is found in moderate numbers in isolated areas, usually associated with the large stands of prickly pear cacti in Atascosa, Wilson, Medina, and Bexar counties. Land use practices and vehicular traffic appear to be the major causes for its current decline in the heavily populated area of Bexar County.

Identification: The carapace in adult Texas tortoises is light to dark brown, whereas in hatchlings it varies from brown to black, with or without light yellow scute centers, and with the marginals edged in yellow. The variable adult plastron pattern consists of irregular, symmetrical scute arrangements in shades of dark brown to yellow. Head and limbs are generally the same color as the carapace, with some dull yellowish or gray pigment, and a broad lighter area along the temporal region of the head.

Pigment on the hatchling plastron is restricted to the seam areas, except on the femoral scutes, where it covers all but the free lateral edges. A yellowish stripe extends from below the corner of the eye to the angle of the jaw, and a light yellow temporal patch is present on the brown head. Juveniles have a creamy white-colored chin and throat. Most scales on the limbs are black, but those on the thigh may be cream to yellow. The top of the tail is gray.

Other features useful for adult identification include *carapace rounded, broad, and domed with flared marginals above the hind limbs; gular scutes elongated, forked, projecting beyond the carapace (upcurved in older males);* nuchal scute usually absent; interhumeral seam longer than intergular seam; pygal region down-curved; grooved scutes on carapace with fine, concentric growth rings that usually surround the lighter yellowish centers; plastron without a hinge; plastron slightly concave in males; bridge well-developed between the carapace and plastron; head narrow, slightly pointed in front; prominent scent glands under the chin in males; front limbs heavily scaled, blunt-clawed; *hind limbs stumpy, elephant-like.*

The only remotely similar species in South Central Texas are the two species of box turtles, the ornate box turtle (*Terrapene ornata ornata*) and the three-toed box turtle (*Terrapene carolina triunguis*), both distinguished by their hinged plastrons and lack of a projecting gular scute.

Size: The carapace length for this species is approximately 6 to 7 inches (15.2 to 17.8 cm), with the record length at about 8³/₄ inches (22.3 cm).

Behavior: Activity periods of the Texas tortoise are controlled by temperature, light, and rain. During the summer this species is usually active in morning and late afternoon hours. According to Rose and Judd (1975), who studied the thermal ecology of *Gopherus berlandieri* in a wild population near Port Isabel, there was a positive correlation between the air temperature and the body temperature of active tortoises, and between substrate temperature and body temperature of those that were inactive. They also noted that when midday temperatures reached 104 F. (40 C.), tortoises limited their activity to the morning and late afternoon. This temperature is considered to be near the critical thermal maximum of 110 F. (42.8 C.) for the species (Rose et al., 1988). During the summer the author has observed more tortoises active during the evening than in the morning in South Central Texas. Tortoises are active after local precipitation begins, but if rain continues for more than 24 hours, they will usually completely disappear. Moreover, tortoises have not been observed from December through February in the South Central Texas region, and thus presumably hibernate in the winter. Voight and Johnson (1976) noted that a warm-up period inside the shelter allows this species to attain full coordination of its functions before the turtle exposes itself. According to Voight and Johnson, this behavior allows it to rapidly escape by returning to shelter when disturbed upon emergence. Voight and Johnson (1977) found that this tortoise's body temperature increases significantly faster than it decreases. When the head is withdrawn into the shell it affords better insulation, thus greatly affecting head-body temperature relationships. The author has noticed that during the day this tortoise spends much of its time in the shade of vegetation, perhaps to reduce prolonged exposure to direct sunlight. This diurnal species spends a majority of its resting time in "pallets" constructed by scraping away soil, ground litter, or wood rat refuse. Pallets are often made near the base of a bush, tuft of grass, or under a large cactus clump. Although it is occasionally found in short burrows in clay soils, the Texas tortoise normally will not dig an extensive burrow. This species has been reported to occupy empty mammal burrows or utilize the large cracks occasionally present in the sandy-loam soils of Wilson County.

126

A tortoise will correct its direction when confronted by obstacles, then assume its previous direction before confronting the object; its movements are oriented by visual and (possibly) olfactory cues. Activity patterns in this species are often not clear, due to temporal, spatial, and social factors that affect the dynamic relationships of their broadly overlapping home ranges. Work done with species of the genus *Gopherus* suggests that they rarely move more than 2 miles from their hatching spot during their lives (Auffenberg and Iverson, 1979). Judd and Rose (1983) found that Texas gopher tortoises do not traverse the entirety of their home ranges on a regular basis. Auffenberg and Weaver (1969) found a density of one tortoise per 82 square meters (98 square yards) on one study grid; another study indicated 10 to 16 tortoises per hectare (2½ acres).

Male tortoises are known to engage in territorial combat. Perhaps the combat in males is for access to females (Judd and Rose, 1983).

Food: This herbivorous tortoise feeds mainly on cactus pads, stems, and grass in the wet season, and additionally, prickly pear fruit in the dry season. Mittleman (1947) reported it subsists during the summer largely on young shoots and highly colored blossoms of a variety of plants. The food supply, of course, determines the growth rate and influences the population density. In captivity, individuals eat lettuce, green pods of black-eyed peas, grass, tomatoes, apples, clover, and other vegetable matter. These tortoises seldom drink, and thus must take moisture from the diet.

Habitat: Gopherus berlandieri is a largely subtropical species of the seasonally dry Gulf coastal plain of southern Texas and northern Mexico, an area characterized by a transition from tropical thorn forest to subtropical scrubland. In Texas, this tortoise prefers sandy, well-drained soils supporting open scrub woodlands, scattered patches of prickly pear (*Opuntia lindheimeri*) and buffalo grass (*Buchloe dactyloides*). It is also found on low hills, and in mesquite, acacia, and chaparral areas throughout the region.

Breeding: Weaver (1970) stated that courtship and mating occur from June to September, and Gunter (1945) observed mating in the spring and fall. Fresh nests have been found in southern Texas from June 8 to September 17 (Auffenberg and Weaver, 1969). Sixty nests were examined by Auffenberg and Weaver; 38 contained 1 egg each, 19 contained 2 eggs each, and 3 had 3 eggs each. Captive females may lay 3 to 4 eggs at a time, with multiple nestings probably occurring during a single season. The granular-surfaced, elongated, hard-shelled, white eggs are 1⁹/₁₆ to 2¹/₈ inches (40 to 54 mm) by 1¹/₈ to 1⁵/₁₆ inches (29 to 34 mm). Eggs are laid in chambers approximately 2¹/₂ inches (60 mm) deep, usually beneath the cover of an overhanging bush. Natural incubation periods range from 88 to 118 days, with hatchlings appearing from August 27 to November 5 (Judd and McQueen, 1980). Newly hatched young are nearly round, 1⁹/₁₆ to 2 inches (40 to 50mm) in carapace length and width. Sexual maturity for females is attained at a carapace length from 6¹/₈ to 6¹/₂ inches (15.5 to 16.5 cm) (Rose and Judd, 1982).

General information: Counting annual growth rings on the epidermal scutes of the carapace will permit the estimation of age of juveniles, but, because of wearing of the scutes, growth rings are generally useless in determining the age of old individuals. In one Texas population, Judd (1982) estimated 4 turtles to each be approximately 52 years old.

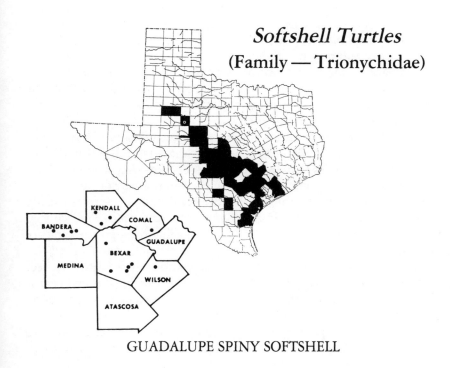

Softshell Turtles
(Family — Trionychidae)

GUADALUPE SPINY SOFTSHELL

Apalone spinifera quadalupensis (Webb) 1962

The highly aquatic softshell turtle family Trionychidae is represented by 14 genera (Meylan, 1987), and 22 species in Africa, Asia, and North America. The generic name has been recently changed from *Trionyx* to *Apalone* (Meylan, 1987), as based on osteological characters and inferred phylogenetic relationships. Softshells have a soft, leathery, and flexible-edged carapace. These short-tempered "greyhounds" of the turtle world can swim very rapidly across muddy river bottoms. *Apalone spinifera* is the most widespread softshell in the New World, ranging from Canada to Mexico; the subspecies, *A. s. guadalupensis,* is endemic to the Colorado, Nueces, and Guadalupe/San Antonio river drainages of Texas.

Identification: This turtle has an oval carapace covered with olive to tan soft, leathery skin, with numerous small white dots over most of its surface, es-

129

pecially anteriorly. Each dot is usually encircled with a narrow black ring. Adult males have white dots that may reach $^1/_{16}$ inch (3 mm) in diameter. Females usually lose their light dots as they age and the carapace becomes mottled. A light border, wider toward the rear, rims the carapace and may be bordered to the inside by a narrow dark line. Its unmarked, hingeless plastron is grayish to white. Head and skin range from olive to tan, and are usually white beneath. Much of the skin surface is covered with numerous small black spots. Two dark-bordered, light stripes lie on each side of the head.

Other characteristics for identification include a *flat, broad, oval, soft, leathery carapace* that is rounded posteriorly and textured with small spiny tubercles that create a sandpaper-like effect when touched. Larger tubercles are more prevalent on the anterior part of the carapace and give the species its common name. Females and juveniles usually only have weakly developed tubercles on the carapace. The reduced bony elements of the carapace are usually visible through the carapace skin covering. Another distinctive characteristic is the *long tubular snout with terminal nostrils.* This turtle has completely webbed, flat feet with three claws on each foot. As in most male turtles, the anal vent is located near the tip of the tail, well beyond the edge of the carapace. No other similar species is found in the area.

Size: The carapace in adult female softshells may reach from 7 to $16^5/_8$ inches (18 to 42.2 cm) long. Adult males are smaller, with a carapace 5 to $8^1/_2$ inches (12.5 to 21.6 cm).

Behavior: The author has observed these fast-moving turtles in captivity for many years, and has noted some interesting behavioral patterns. When food was placed in an aquarium, the softshell generally responded faster than did other aquatic turtles in the tank. When other species of turtles of a similar size were in the tank (such as the common musk turtle, yellow mud turtle, red-eared slider, and Texas river cooter), the softshell appeared to be rather tolerant, allowing the other turtles to crawl over its carapace.

A softshell turtle will often bury itself in a layer of shallow mud or sand, leaving only the eyes, snout, and nostrils exposed. Conant (1975) reported that this species aestivates in mud during periods of drought. During hibernation they do not surface to breathe air, but rather meet their respiratory needs by gaseous exchanges through the skin, cloaca, and throat lining. When thermoregulating, softshell turtles are known to heat twice as fast as they cool (Smith et al., 1981).

Food: Primarily carnivorous, these turtles feed on insects, snails, aquatic invertebrates, crawfish, fish, frogs, and some vegetation. In captivity, they may take a variety of foods, including fish, raw beef, and molluscs.

Habitat: These almost strictly aquatic turtles are found in permanent waters throughout South Central Texas. They inhabit lakes and large marsh-like ponds near rivers and streams, and it is not unusual to see one basking on the edge of banks, sandbars, logs, or stacks of debris on the bank. Such sites always have quick access to the water.

Breeding: This subspecies nests from late May through July. The female usually digs a 6- to 8-inch (15.3 to 20.3 cm) deep cavity into the loose soil of a bank in an area usually exposed to the sun near the water's edge. One or more clutches of at least 20 or more thin-shelled, brittle, spherical eggs are laid each season. These eggs are 1 to $1^{3}/_{16}$ inches (25 to 30 mm) in diameter. Incubation periods vary from 60 to 75 days, depending on environmental conditions. The sex of hatchling soft-shelled turtles is not determined by the incubation temperature of the eggs (Bull and Vogt, 1979).

General information: This species has lived in captivity for at least 25 years. If this turtle is handled, care should be taken that the long, flexible neck does not extend around to let the head bite the handler.

Glossary

aestivate — to become dormant during periods of heat and drought.

agonistic — related to or being aggressive or defensive social interaction between individuals usually of the same species, e.g., fighting, fleeing, or submitting.

aldrin — an exceedingly poisonous cyclodiene insecticide.

amphipods — a group of small, predominantly aquatic crustaceans.

annelid — an elongated, segmented invertebrate such as an earthworm or a leech, belonging to the phylum Annelida.

anus — an external opening of the cloaca for elimination of wastes.

aquatic — growing or living in, or frequenting, water.

arachnid — a class of 8-legged arthropod invertebrates including spiders, scorpions, ticks, and mites.

arboreal — inhabiting or frequenting trees.

areolan tubercle — a raised, rounded, knot-like projection on the carapace of a turtle.

arthropod — invertebrate animal with jointed legs and exoskeleton of the phylum Arthropoda; includes insects, arachnids, and crustaceans.

ataxia — an inability to coordinate the voluntary muscular movements; symptomatic of some nervous disorders.

axilla — the armpit.

barbels — small skin projections that hang downward from the throat and chin of turtles.

biotas — the plants and animals of a region.

bridge — the bony arch connection on either side of the turtle's shell that connects the carapace and plastron.

carapace — the top section of the turtle shell.

carnivorous — subsisting or feeding on animal tissues.

caudal — of, or relating to, the tail.

cloacal — referring to the chamber into which the urinary, digestive, and reproductive canals discharge their contents; opens to the outside of the body by the anus.

concave — hollowed or rounded inward, like the inside of a bowl.

133

concentric — having a common center.

copulate — to engage in sexual intercourse.

costal scutes — large scutes running down each side of the carapace (usually four).

crustaceans — members of the arthropod phylum (class Crustacea), composed of mostly aquatic arthropods and including amphipods, isopods, and decapods.

dewlap — a laterally compressed, vertical fold of skin on the throat of some lizards.

dieldrin — a white crystalline chlorinated hydrocarbon insecticide which persists in the environment.

Diptera — an insect order that includes flies and mosquitoes.

diurnal — active during the daytime.

dorsal — related to or situated near the back or upper part of the body.

dorsolateral — situated between the sides and top of the back.

ectoparasite — parasite that lives on the exterior of the host.

edaphic — resulting from, pertaining to, or influenced by soil conditions.

elliptical — of, relating to, or shaped as an oval.

endemic — restricted to occurrence in a specified geographic area.

epidermal scutes — scutes arising from the outer epithelial layer of the external surface.

femoral pore — found in a row on the ventral surface of the thigh in many lizards; a relatively deep pit in the center of a usually enlarged, single scale.

femoral scutes — the fifth or ultimate pair of laminae on the plastron of turtles.

flexible groove — a flexible, elongated depression channeled between 2 folds.

follicle — a small sac, cavity, or gland.

frontal scale — the large, median, unpaired plate on top of the head between the eyes in lizards and snakes.

frontonasal scale — a head scale or scales in reptiles located between the internasals, prefrontals, and loreals (typical of many lizards and turtles).

gastropods — slugs and snails; members of the mollusc phylum.

genus — a category in the hierarchy of biological classification that ranks between the family and the species, comprising structurally or phylogenetically related species or a single species exhibiting unusual differentiation.

gonad — any organ in animals in which ova or spermatozoa are formed.

granular — having a grainy texture.

gravid — carrying eggs or young (pregnant).

groin — the angle formed by the anterior margin of the hind limb and body; slight depression or cavity at the insertion of the hind limb.

growth rings — the rings found on scutes of the carapace on many turtles.

134

For turtles found in cold climates growth proceeds in cycles, and a wrinkle is formed around the edge of the scute as growth ceases during the winter. Thus, the age of some turtles may be calculated by counting the number of rings around each scute.

gular fold — a transverse fold of skin across the throat immediately anterior to the intersection of the forelegs.

gular scutes — the front scutes of a turtle plastron, usually paired but sometimes single.

gulars — the scales on the throat or gular fold of lizards.

Hemiptera — the insect order of "true bugs," including water boatmen, back swimmers, assassin bugs, and stinkbugs.

hibernaculum — a shelter occupied during winter by an inactive or dormant animal.

herbivores — plant-eating animals.

home range — as used here, a term given to the area in which an animal normally lives, regardless of whether or not the area is defended as a territory.

Hymenoptera — the insect order that includes ants, wasps, and bees.

hyoid — the bone or cartilaginous structure in the floor of the mouth which supports the tongue.

insectivorous — depending on insects for food.

intergular scute — small scute (occasionally present) which separates, or partially separates, the gular scutes.

interhumeral seam — the seam running between the humeral scutes.

interorbital scales — small scales that are between orbits on the dorsal surface of the head. These scales are often bound on the outside by semicircular rows of scales that border the supraocular series of scales.

isopod — any of a large order of small crustaceans with seven thoracic segments, each bearing a pair of similar legs; includes the "pill bug."

keel — a longitudinal ridge on the upper or lower section of some turtles, or referring to scales with an elevated detectable ridge (on lizards).

labial scales — the scales on lips that border the mouth in reptiles.

lamella — thin plate or scale, typically of bone or keratin.

laminae — the upper or epidermal plates of the shell in turtles.

Lepidoptera — the insect order that includes butterflies and moths.

lobe — a somewhat rounded projection or division of a bodily organ.

marginal scutes — the small scutes around the edge of the carapace.

median stripe — longitudinal stripe in the middle of the back or belly.

middorsal — of, or pertaining to, the center of the back.

molluscs — the phylum of invertebrates that includes clams, octopuses, snails, and slugs.

nape — the back of the neck.

nocturnal — active at night.

nuchal — of, or pertaining to, an unpaired scute on the carapace in turtles, or 1 or 2 pair of enlarged dorsal scales on the neck just posterior to the enlarged dorsal scales of the head in skinks.

omnivores — animals that eat both vegetable and animal material.

orbit — the area or bony cavity containing the eye.

Orthoptera — insect order that includes grasshoppers, katydids, crickets, mantids, walking sticks, and roaches.

osteoderms — the bony deposits in the form of a plate or scale found in the dermal layers of the skin in some reptiles.

ova — female gametes; eggs.

ovarian — of, relating to, or involving an ovary (an essential female reproductive organ that produces eggs and female sex hormones).

oviparous — producing young by laying eggs that develop outside of the body.

oviposition — the act of laying eggs.

ovulation — the act of producing eggs or discharging them from an ovary.

paravertebral — lying on each or either side of the middorsal or vertebral line.

parietal — large plates on the upper surface of the head just behind the frontal or the frontoparietals.

parthenogenetically — development of eggs and embryos without fertilization by a male.

photoperiod — a recurring cycle of light and dark periods of a given length.

plastron — ventral part of the shell of a turtle, consisting of paired epidermal shields and underlying bone.

postanal plate — one of the pair of large plates found behind the anus in males of some lizard species; generally lying against the posterior wall of a pocket.

postantebrachial scales — scales on the posterior surface (toward the elbow) of the forelimbs (usually found in teiid lizards).

postmental scales — scales lying along the midventral line posterior to the mental scale.

postnasal scale — a small scale or scales on the side of the head, just in front of the loreal scale.

postrostral scale — a small scale or scales bordering the rostral posteriorly, anterior to the internasals (in many lizards).

preanal scale — any one of the row of scales immediately preceding the anal opening in lizards.

prehensile — adapted for grasping or wrapping around.

pygal — the posteriormost bone on the middorsal line of the turtle carapace.

riparian — relating to, or living in, the habitat zone along a natural watercourse.

rostral scale — the scale at the tip of the snout, bordering the mouth, and separating the left/right rows of supralabial scales.

saxicolous — inhabiting or growing among rocks.

scute — an enlarged scale, plate, or lamina; usually referring to the scales on the turtle shell.

seam — the line of contact between two scutes or laminae on the turtle's shell.

snout-vent length — the measured distance between the tip of the snout and the vent or anus.

species — a minimal category in the hierarchy of biological classification ranking immediately below the genus comprising populations of organisms capable of interbreeding.

spermatogenetic cycle — the process of male gamete formation, from meiosis to the production of spermatozoa.

spherical — having the form of a sphere (globe).

subcaudal scale — a scale lying on the ventral side of the tail in reptiles.

subspecies — a trinomial taxonomic category that ranks immediately below species, designating a morphologically recognizable and/or geographically isolated series of populations. Subspecies typically have a discrete geographic range, and interbreed with other subspecies of the same species where their ranges contact or overlap. Such interbreeding produces intermediates, termed "intergrades."

supracaudals — the laminae on the turtle's carapace or a structure on the dorsal surface of the tail.

supraocular scales — the scales lying on the dorsum of the orbit in lizards.

synonymy — a list of different names that have been applied to identical subspecies, species, or genera. For a taxonomist to have a name placed in or removed from a synonymy is usually based on biological evidence, and is subject to subsequent acceptance or rejection by other taxonomists.

syntype — from 1 or 2 to several original specimens used in describing a new species, a practice employed often by nineteenth-century taxonomists. Modern taxonomy calls for a single type specimen to be designated when a new species or subspecies is described (the holotype) and allows for a taxonomist reviewing previous work utilizing syntypes to select one of them as the type (a lectotype).

taxa — any taxonomic category, e.g., species, genus variety.

taxonomy — the theory and practice of classifying organisms into the Linnaean hierarchy of categories (class, family, genus, species, etc.).

terrestrial — land-inhabiting or ground-dwelling.

testes — male reproductive organ that produces spermatozoa and male sex hormones.

testicular — referring to the testes.

torpor — extreme sluggishness or stagnation of function.

tubercles — small, rounded bumps or knobs on the skin.

tympanum — the eardrum; the membrane covering the external opening of the middle ear chamber.

type locality — the place where the original (type) specimen of a species or subspecies was collected.

ubiquitous — widespread.

vent — the anal opening; the external opening of the cloaca.

ventral — of, or pertaining to, the lower surface.

vernacular — the common native speech applied to a plant or animal, as distinguished from the binomial Latin nomenclature for species names.

vertebral keel — a keel along the central dorsal scutes.

vertebral line — a row of scales or other structure lying middorsally in a longitudinal fashion.

viviparous — producing living young by means of eggs that are implanted in some form of placenta, permitting the exchange of materials between mother and fetus.

Bibliography

Andrews, R. M. 1985. "Oviposition Frequency of *Anolis carolinensis.*" *Copeia* 1985(1):259–262.

Auffenberg, W., and J. B. Iverson. 1979. "Demography of Terrestrial Turtles." Pp. 541–569 in *Turtles, Perspectives and Research,* edited by H. Morlock and M. Harless. New York: John Wiley & Sons.

Auffenberg, W., and W. G. Weaver, Jr. 1969. "*Gopherus berlandieri* in Southeastern Texas." *Bull. Florida St. Mus.* 13(3):141–203.

Avery, R. A. 1979. "Lizards — A Study in Thermoregulation." *Institute of Biology. Studies in Biology:* No. 109.

Axtell, R. W. 1950. "Notes on a Specimen of *Sceloporus poinsettii* and Its Young." *Herpetologica* 6(3):80–81.

———. 1956. "A Solution to the Long Neglected *Holbrookia lacerata* problem, and the Description of Two New Subspecies of *Holbrookia.*" *Bull. Chicago Acad. Sci.* 10(11):163–179.

———. 1959. "Amphibians and Reptiles of the Black Gap Wildlife Management Area, Brewster County, Texas." *Southwest Nat.* 4(2):88–109.

———. 1960. "Orientation by *Holbrookia maculata* (Lacertilia, Iguanidae) to Solar and Reflected Heat." *Southwest. Nat.* 5(1):45–47.

———. 1981. "*Holbrookia propinqua:* Type Specimens, Collector, His Route, and Restriction of Locality, with Comments on Baird's '*Reptiles of the Boundary*' as an Important Taxonomic Reference." *J. Herp.* 15(2):211–217.

———. 1986. *Interpretive Atlas of Texas Lizards: Coleonyx brevis.* (Published by author).

———. 1987. *Interpretive Atlas of Texas Lizards: Sceloporus poinsettii.* (Published by author).

Axtell, R. W., and A. O. Wasserman. 1953. "Interesting Herpetological Records from Southern Texas and Northern Mexico." *Herpetologica* 9(1):1–6.

Baird, S. F. 1859. "Reptiles of the Boundary." 24 pp. in *Report on the United States and Mexican Boundary Survey,* Vol. II, Pt. II, Made Under the Direction of the Secretary of the Interior by William H. Emory. Washington: C. Wendell.

Ballinger, R. E. 1971. "Comparative Demography of Two Viviparous Lizards (*Sceloporus jarrovi* and *Sceloporus poinsettii*) with Consideration of the Evolutionary Ecology of Viviparity in Lizards." *Diss. Abstr. Int.* B32(8):4540–4541.

———. 1973. "Comparative Demography of Two Viviparous Iguanid Lizards (*Sceloporus jarrovi* and *Sceloporus poinsettii*)." *Ecology* 54(2):269–283.

———. 1973. "Experimental Evidence of the Tail as a Balancing Organ in the Lizard, *Anolis carolinensis*." *Herpetologica* 29(1):65–66.

———. 1974. "Reproduction of the Texas Horned Lizard, *Phrynosoma cornutum*." *Herpetologica* 30(4):321–327.

———. 1977. "Reproductive Strategies: Food Availability as a Source of Proximal Variation in a Lizard." *Ecology* 58(3):628–635.

Ballinger, R. E., and D. R. Clark, Jr. 1973. "Energy Content of Lizard Eggs and the Measurement of Reproductive Effort." *J. Herp.* 7(2):129–132.

Ballinger, R. E., and T. G. Hipp. 1985. "Hematological Variations in the Collared Lizard, *Crotaphytus collaris* (Sauria: Iguanidae)." *Copeia* 1985(3):782–784.

———. 1985. "Reproduction in the Collared Lizard, *Crotaphytus collaris,* in West Central Texas." *Copeia* 1985(4):976–980.

Ballinger, R. E., and G. D. Shrank. 1970 "Acclimation Rate and Variability of the Critical Thermal Maximum in the Lizard *Phrynosoma cornutum*." *Physiol. Zool.* 43(1):19–22.

———. 1972. "Reproductive Potential of Female Whiptail Lizards, *Cnemidophorus gularis gularis*." *Herpetologica* 28(3):217–222.

Ballinger, R. E., and D. W. Tinkle. 1979. "On the Cost of Tail Regeneration to Body Growth in Lizards." *J. Herp.* 13 (3): 374–375.

Ballinger, R. E., E. D. Tyler, and D. W. Tinkle. 1972. "Reproductive Ecology of a West Texas Population of the Greater Earless Lizard, *Cophosaurus texanus*." *Amer. Midl. Nat.* 88(2):419–428.

Baxter, D. 1971. "Lizards." *Texas Parks & Wildlife* 29(11):24–27.

Beasom, S. L. 1974. "Selectivity of Predator Control Techniques in South Texas." *J. Wildlife Mgt.* 38(4):837–844.

Begon, M. 1979. *Investigating Animal Abundance: Capture-Recapture for Biologists.* Baltimore, Maryland: University Park Press.

Behler, J. L., and F. W. King. 1979. *The Audubon Society Field Guide to North American Reptiles and Amphibians.* New York: Alfred A. Knopf.

Belfit, S. C., and V. F. Belfit. 1985. "Notes on the Ecology of a Population of *Eumeces obsoletus* (Scincidae) in New Mexico." *Southwest Nat.* 30(4):612–614.

Bertl, J., and F. C. Killebrew. 1983. "An Osteological Comparison of *Graptemys caglei* Haynes and McKown and *Graptemys versa* Stejneger (Testu-

140

dines: Emydidae)." *Herpetologica* 39(4):375–382.

Best, T. L., and G. S. Pfaffenberger. 1987. "Age and Sexual Variation in the Diet of Collared Lizards (*Crotaphytus collaris*)." *Southwest. Nat.* 32(4):415–426.

Best, T. L., and P. J. Polechla. 1983. "Foods of the Texas Spotted Whiptail Lizard (*Cnemidophorus gularis*) in New Mexico." *Southwest. Nat.* 28(3):376.

Bethea, N. J. 1972. "Effects of Temperature on Heart Rate and Rates of Cooling and Warming in *Terrapene ornata*." *Comp. Biochem. Physiol.* 41A:301–305.

Bider, J. R. 1962. "Dynamics and the Temporo-Spatial Relations of a Vertebrate Community." *Ecology* 43(4):634–646.

Bigony, M. 1981. "When Was the Last Time You Saw a Horned Lizard?" *Texas Parks & Wildlife* 39(2):28–31.

Blair, A. P. 1950. "Notes on Two Anguid Lizards." *Copeia* 1950(1):57.

Blair, W. F. 1950. "The Biotic Provinces of Texas." *Texas J. Sci.* 2(1):93–117.

———. 1960. *The Rusty Lizard: A Population Study.* Austin: University of Texas Press.

———. 1976. "Some Aspects of the Biology of the Ornate Box Turtle, *Terrapene ornata*." *Southwest. Nat.* 21(1):89–104.

Blaney, R. M., and P. J. Kimmich. 1973. "Notes on the Young of the Texas Horned Lizard, *Phrynosoma cornutum*." *HISS-News Journal* 1(4):120.

Boulenger, G. A. 1897. "A Revision of the Lizards of the Genus *Sceloporus*." *Proc. Zool. Soc. London* 1897:474–522.

Bowen, G. S. 1977. "Prolonged Western Equine Encephalitis Viremia in the Texas Tortoise (*Gopherus berlandieri*)." *Amer. J. Trop. Med. Hyg.* 26(1):171–175.

Bowers, C. C., and H. M. Smith. 1947. "Hibernation of Lizards in Western Texas." *Herpetologica* 4:80.

Bowker, R. G. 1980. "Sound Production in *Cnemidophorus gularis*." *J. Herp.* 14(2):187–188.

Bowler, J. K. 1977. *Longevity of Reptiles and Amphibians in North American Collections.* Society for the Study of Amphibians and Reptiles and Philadelphia Herpetological Society.

Bramble, D. M. 1974. "Occurrence and Significance of the Os Transiliens in Gopher Tortoises." *Copeia* 1974(1):102–109.

———. 1982. "*Scaptochelys:* Generic Revision and Evolution of Gopher Tortoises." *Copeia* 1982(4):852–867.

Brattstrom, B. H. 1952. "Diurnal Activities of a Nocturnal Animal." *Herpetologica* 8(3):61–63.

Breckenridge, W. J. 1943. "The Life History of the Black-banded Skink *Eumeces septentrionalis septentrionalis* (Baird)." *Amer. Midl. Nat.* 29(3):591–

606.

Brewer, K., and F. C. Killebrew. 1986. "The Annual Testicular Cycle of *Pseudemys scripta elegans* (Emydidae) in the Texas Panhandle." *Southwest. Nat.* 31(3):299–305.

Brimley, C. S. 1910. "Records of Some Reptiles and Batrachians from the Southeastern United States." *Proc. Biol. Soc. Wash.* 23:9–18.

Brooks, G. R., Jr. 1967. "Population Ecology of the Ground Skink, *Lygosoma laterale* (Say)." *Ecol. Monographs* 37(2):71–87.

Brown, B. C. 1950. *An Annotated Check List of the Reptiles and Amphibians of Texas.* Waco, Texas: Baylor Univ. Studies.

———. 1951. "*Eumeces anthracinus* in Texas." *Herpetologica* 7(2):76.

———. 1951. "A Range Extension of the Southern Prairie Skink in Texas." *Herpetologica* 7(2):72.

Brown, B. C., and J. Haver. 1952. "An Unusually Large Congregation of Turtles." *Herpetologica* 8(1):2.

Brown, D. A. 1964. "Nesting of a Captive *Gopherus berlandieri* (Agassiz)." *Herpetologica* 20(3):209–210.

Brown, E. E. 1956. "Nests and Young of the Six-lined Racerunner *Cnemidophorus sexlineatus* Linnaeus." *J. Mitchell Soc.* 72:30–40.

Brown, T. L., and R. V. Lucchino. 1971. "A Record-sized Specimen of the Texas Horned Lizard (*Phrynosoma cornutum*)." *Texas J. Sci.* 24(3):353–54.

Bull, J. J. 1980. "Sex Determination in Reptiles." *Q. Rev. Biol.* 55(1):3–21.

———. 1985. "Non-temperature Dependent Sex Determination in Two Suborders of Turtles." *Copeia* 1985(3):784–786.

Bull, J. J., and R. C. Vogt. 1979. "Temperature-Dependent Sex Determination in Turtles." *Science* 206:1186–1188.

Bull, J. J., R. C. Vogt, and C. J. McCoy. 1982. "Sex Determining Temperatures in Turtles: a Geographic Comparison." *Evolution* 36:326–332.

Burger, W. L., P. W. Smith, and H. M. Smith. 1949. "Notable Records of Reptiles and Amphibians in Oklahoma, Arkansas, and Texas." *J. Tenn. Acad. Sci.* 24(2):130–134.

Burkett, R. D. 1962. "Two Clutches of Eggs in the Lizard, *Gerrhonotus liocephalus infernalis*." *Herpetologica* 18(3):211.

———. 1966. "An Extension of Known Range in Texas for the Stinkpot Turtle, *Sternothaerus odoratus*." *Trans. Kansas Acad. Sci.* 69(3–4):361.

Burrage, B. R. 1964. "Two Longevity Records for *Anolis carolinensis carolinensis*. Voigt." *Herpetologica* 20:140.

Burt, C. E. 1928. "The Synonymy, Variation, and Distribution of the Collared Lizard, *Crotaphytus collaris* (Say)." *Occ. Papers Mus. Zool. Univ. Mich.* 196:1–19.

———. 1929. "The Synonymy, Variation, and Distribution of the Sonoran Skink, *Eumeces obsoletus* (Baird and Girard)." *Occ. Papers Mus. Zool. Univ. Mich.* 201:1–12.

————. 1931. "On the Occurrence of a Throat-fan in *Callisaurus ventralis gabbii* and Two Species of *Crotaphytus.*" *Copeia* 1931(2):58.

————. 1931. "The Status of the Spotted Race-runner, *Cnemidophorus sexlineatus gularis* (Baird and Girard)." *Proc. Biol. Soc. Wash.* 44:73–78.

————. 1936. "Contributions to Texan Herpetology. V. Spiny and Scaly Lizards (Sceloporus)." *Papers Mich. Acad. Sci. Arts, Ltrs.* 22:533–540.

————. 1937. "The Lizards of the Southeastern United States." *Trans. Kansas Acad. Sci.* 40:349–366.

Burt, C. E., and M. D. Burt. 1929. "Field Notes and Locality Records on a Collection of Amphibians and Reptiles Chiefly from the Western Half of the United States." *J. Wash. Acad. Sci.* 19(20):448–460.

Bury, R. B., and E. L. Smith. 1986. "Aspects of the Ecology and Management of the Tortoise *Gopherus berlandieri* at Laguna Atascosa, Texas." *Southwest. Nat.* 31(3):387–394.

Bustard, H. R. 1967. "Gekkonid Lizards Adapt Fat Storage to Desert Environments." *Science* 158:1197–1198.

Buth, D. G., G. C. Gorman, and C. S. Lieb. 1980. "Genetic Divergence Between *Anolis carolinensis* and its Cuban Progenitor, *Anolis porcatus.*" *J. Herp.* 14(3):279–284.

Cagle, F. R. 1950. "Notes on *Holbrookia texana* in Texas." *Copeia* 1950(3):230.

Cahn, A. R. 1962. "The Breeding Habits of the Texas Horned Toad, *Phrynosoma cornutum.*" *Amer. Nat.* 60:546–551.

Carpenter, C. C. 1960. "Reproduction in Oklahoma *Sceloporus* and *Cnemidophorus.*" *Herpetologica* 16:175–182.

————. 1978. "Comparative Display Behavior in the Genus *Sceloporus* (Iguanidae)." *Milwaukee Publ. Mus. Contr. Biol. Geol.* 18:1–71.

Carr, A. F., Jr. 1938. "Notes on the *Pseudemys scripta* complex." *Herpetologica* 1(5):131–135.

————. 1952. *Handbook of Turtles.* Ithaca, New York: Comstock.

Carr, J. L., and T. W. Houseal. 1981. "Post-hibernation Behavior in *Terrapene carolina triunguis* (Emydidae)." *Southwest. Nat.* 26(2):199–220.

Cavazos, L. F. 1951. "Spermatogenesis of the Horned Lizard *Phrynosoma cornutum.*" *Amer. Nat.* 85:373–379.

Chaney, A. H., and R. E. Gordon. 1954. "Notes on a Population of *Sceloporus merriami merriami* Stejneger." *Texas J. Sci.* 6(1):78–82.

Christian, K. A., C. R. Tracy, and W. P. Porter. 1986. "The Effect of Cold Exposure During Incubation of *Sceloporus undulatus* Eggs." *Copeia* 1986(4):1012–1014.

Christiansen, J. L., and J. A. Cooper. 1984. "Reproduction of *Kinosternon flavescens* (Kinosternidae) in Iowa." *Southwest. Nat.* 29(3):349.

Christiansen, J. L., and A. E. Dunham. 1972. "Reproduction of the Yellow Mud Turtle, *Kinosternon flavescens flavescens* in New Mexico." *Herpetologica* 28:130–137.

Christiansen, J. L., and B. J. Gallaway. 1984. "Raccoon Removal, Nesting Success, and Hatchling Emergence in Iowa Turtles with Special Reference to *Kinosternon flavescens* (Kinosternidae)." *Southwest. Nat.* 29(3):343.

Christiansen, J. L., J. A. Cooper, J. W. Bickham, B. J. Gallaway, and M. D. Springer. 1985. "Aspects of the Natural History of the Yellow Mud Turtle *Kinosternon flavescens* (Kinosternidae) in Iowa: A Proposed Endangered Species." *Southwest. Nat.* 30(3):413–425.

Clark, D. B., and J. W. Gibbons. 1969. "Dietary Shift in the Turtle *Pseudemys scripta* (Schoepff) from Youth to Maturity." *Copeia* 1969 (4):704–706.

Clark, D. R., Jr. 1971. "Branding as a Marking Technique for Amphibians and Reptiles." *Copeia* 1971(1):148–151.

———. 1976. "Ecological Observations on a Texas Population of Six-Lined Racerunners, *Cnemidophorus sexlineatus* (Reptilia, Lacertilia, Teiidae)." *J. Herp.* 10(2):133–138.

Clark, D. R., Jr., and J. C. Kroll. 1974. "Thermal Ecology of Anoline Lizards: Temperature Versus Tropical Strategies." *Southwest. Nat.* 19 (1):9–19.

Clarke, R. F. 1965. "An Ethological Study of the Iguanid Lizard Genera *Callisaurus, Cophosaurus* and *Holbrookia*." *Emporia State Res. Stud.* 13(4):1–66.

Cole, C. J. 1972. "Chromosome Variation in North American Fence Lizards (Genus *Sceloporus; undulatus* Species Group)." *Syst. Zool.* 21(4):357–363.

———. 1978. "Karotypes and Systematics of the Lizards in the *variabilis, jalapae,* and *scalaris* Species Groups of the Genus *Sceloporus*." *Amer. Museum Novitates* 2653:1–13.

Collins, J. T. 1982. *Amphibians and Reptiles in Kansas.* 2nd ed. Lawrence, Kansas: Univ. Kansas Publ. Mus. Nat. Hist.

Collins, J. T., R. Conant, J. E. Huheey, J. L. Knight, E. M. Rundquist, and H. M. Smith. 1982. *Standard Common and Current Scientific Names for North American Amphibians and Reptiles.* 2nd ed. Lawrence, Kansas: Society for the Study of Amphibians and Reptiles.

Committee on Resources in Herpetology. 1975. *Collections of Preserved Amphibians and Reptiles in the United States.* Lawrence, Kansas: Society for the Study of Amphibians and Reptiles.

Conant, R. 1975. *A Field Guide to the Reptiles and Amphibians of Eastern and Central North America.* Boston: Houghton Mifflin Co.

Conant, R., and J. F. Berry. 1978. "Turtles of the Family Kinosternidae in the Southwestern United States and Adjacent Mexico: Identification and Distribution." *Amer. Museum Novitates* 2642:1–18.

Conant, R., and K. G. Hudson. 1949. "Longevity Records for Reptiles and Amphibians in the Philadelphia Zoological Garden." *Herpetologica* 5:1–8.

Cook, F. A. 1943. "Alligators and Lizards of Mississippi." *Miss. Game and Fish Comm. Survey Bull.* 5:pp.v + 20 (mimeo).

Cook, R. S., D. O. Trainer, W. C. Glazener, and B. D. Nassif. 1965. "A Seriological Study of Infectious Diseases of Wild Populations in South Texas." *Trans. N. Amer. Wildlife Natl. Res. Conf.* 13:142–155.

Cooper, W. E., Jr. 1984. "Female Secondary Sexual Coloration and Sex Recognition in the Keeled Earless Lizard, *Holbrookia propinqua.*" *Anim. Behav.* 32:1142–1150.

———. 1985. "Female Residency and Courtship Intensity in a Territorial Lizard, *Holbrookia propinqua.*" *Amphibia-Reptilia* 6:63–69.

———. 1986. "Chromatic Components of Female Secondary Sexual Coloration: Influence on Social Behavior of Male Keeled Earless Lizards (*Holbrookia propinqua*)." *Copeia* 1986 (4):980–986.

Cooper, W. E., Jr., and R. F. Clarke. 1982. "Steriodal Induction of Female Reproductive Coloration in the Keeled Earless Lizard, *Holbrookia propinqua.*" *Herpetologica* 38(3):425–429.

Cooper, W. E., Jr., C. S. Adams, and J. L. Dobie. 1983. "Female Color Change in the Keeled Earless Lizard, *Holbrookia propinqua:* Relationship to the Reproductive Cycle." *Southwest Nat.* 28(3):275–280.

Cope, E. D. 1974. *The Osteology of the Lacertilia.* Reprint. Lawrence, Kansas: Society for the Study of Amphibians and Reptiles.

Cowles, R. B. 1977. *Desert Journal Reflections of a Naturalist.* California: Univ. Calif. Press.

Crews, D. 1974. "Effects of Group Stability, Male-male Aggression, and Male Courtship Behaviour on Environmentally-induced Ovarian Recrudescence in the Lizard *Anolis carolinensis.*" *J. Zool. Lond.* 172:419–441.

Crowley, S. R. 1985. "Insensitivity to Desiccation of Sprint Running Performance in the Lizard, *Sceloporus undulatus.*" *J. Herp.* 19(1):171–174.

———. 1987. "The Effect of Desiccation upon the Preferred Body Temperature and Activity Level of the Lizard *Sceloporus undulatus.*" *Copeia* 1987(1):25–32.

Cuellar, O. 1966. "Oviducal Anatomy and Sperm Storage Structures in Lizards." *J. Morph.* 119:7–20.

Culley, D. D., Jr., and H. G. Applegate. 1967. "Pesticides at Presidio. IV. Reptiles, Birds, and Mammals." *Texas J. Sci.* 19(3):301–310.

Dalquest, W. W. 1962. "Tortoises from the Pliocene of Texas." *Texas J. Sci.* 14(2):192–196.

Davis, W. B. 1945. "The Hatching of *Leiolopisma laterale.*" *Copeia* 1945(2):115–116.

———. 1974. "The Mediterranean Gecko, *Hemidactylus turcicus* in Texas." *J. Herp.* 8(1):77–80.

Davis, W. B., and J. R. Dixon. 1958. "A New *Coleonyx* from Texas." *Proc. Biol. Soc. Wash.* 71:149–152.

Degenhardt, W. G. 1966. "A Method of Counting Some Diurnal Ground Lizards of the Genera *Holbrookia* and *Cnemidophorus* with Results from the Big Bend National Park." *Amer. Midl. Nat.* 75(1):61–100.

145

Dial, B. E. 1975. "Aspects of the Ecology and Systematics of the Lizards *Coleonyx brevis* and *Coleonyx reticulatus* (Lacertilia; Gekkonidae). Master's thesis, Texas A&M University, College Station. 211 pp.

————. 1978. "Aspects of the Behavioral Ecology of Two Chihuahuan Desert Geckos (Reptilia; Lacertilia; Gekkonidae)." *J. Herp.* 12(2):209–216.

————. 1978. "The Thermal Ecology of Two Sympatric, Nocturnal *Coleonyx* (Lacertilia: Gekkonidae)." *Herpetologica* 34(2):194–201.

————. 1986. "Tail Display in Two Species of Iguanid Lizards: A Test of the 'Predator Signal' Hypothesis." *Amer. Nat.* 127(1):103–111.

Dial, B. E., and L. C. Fitzpatrick. 1981. "The Energetic Costs of Tail Autotomy to Reproduction in the Lizard *Coleonyx brevis* (Sauria: Gekkonidae)." *Oecologia* 51:310–317.

————. 1982. "Evaporative Water Loss in Sympatric *Coleonyx* (Sauria: Gekkonidae)." *Comp. Biochem. Physiol.* 71A(4):623–625.

————. 1983. "Lizard Tail Autotomy: Function and Energetics of Postautotomy Tail Movement in *Scincella lateralis*." *Science* 219(4583):391–393.

Dixon, J. R. 1958. "The Warty Gecko from Laredo, Texas." *Herpetologica* 13(4):256.

————. 1960. "Epizoophytic Algae on Some Turtles of Texas and Mexico." *Texas J. Sci.* 12(1–2):36–38.

————. 1987. *Amphibians and Reptiles of Texas.* College Station: Texas A&M University Press.

Duellman, W. E., and R. G. Zweifel. 1962. "A Synopsis of the Lizards of the *sexlineatus* Group (Genus *Cnemidophorus*)." *Bull. Amer. Mus. Nat. Hist.* 123:159–210.

Dunham, A. E. 1980. "An Experimental Study of Interspecific Competition Between the Iguanid Lizards *Sceloporus merriami* and *Urosaurus ornatus*." *Ecol. Monographs* 50(3):309–330.

————. 1982. "Demographic and Life-History Variation Among Populations of the Iguanid Lizard *Urosaurus ornatus:* Implications for the Study of Life-History Phenomena in Lizards." *Herpetologica* 38(1):208–221.

————. 1983. "Realized Niche Overlap, Resource Abundance, and Intensity of Interspecific Competition." Pp. 261–280 in *Lizard Ecology: Studies of a Model Organism,* edited by R. B. Huey, E. R. Pianka, and T. W. Schoener. Cambridge, Massachusetts: Harvard University Press.

Dunson, W. A. 1982. "Low Water Vapor Conductance of Hard-shelled Eggs of the Gecko Lizards *Hemidactylus* and *Lepidodactylus*." *J. Exp. Zool.* 219:377–379.

————. 1986. "Estuarine Populations of the Snapping Turtle (*Chelydra*) as a Model for the Evolution of Marine Adaptations in Reptiles." *Copeia* 1986(3):741–756.

Dutton, R. H., and L. C. Fitzpatrick. 1975. "Metabolic Compensation to

Seasonal Temperatures in the Rusty Lizard, *Sceloporus olivaceus.*" *Comp. Biochem. Physiol.* 51A:309–318.

Eads, R. B., G. C. Menzies, and B. G. Hightower. 1956. "The Ticks of Texas, with Notes on Their Medical Significance." *Texas J. Sci.* 8(1):7–24.

Easterla, D. A. 1975. "Giant Desert Centipede Preys upon Snake." *Southwest. Nat.* 20(3):411.

Edwards, C. L. 1896. "Life Habits of *Phrynosoma.*" *Science* 3(73):763–765.

———. 1903. "A Note on *Phrynosoma.*" *Science* 17(438):826–827.

Elliott, W. R. 1977. "An Annotated Checklist of the Reptiles and Amphibians of the U.T.S.A. Campus." (Unpublished paper.)

———, et al. 1978. *Niche Partitioning Between Three Species of the Genus Sceloporus (Lacertilia, Iguanidae) on the U.T.S.A. Campus.* U.T.S.A.: College of Sciences & Mathematics.

Ellis, T. K. 1940. "Notes on Behavior of *Anolis.*" *Copeia* 1940(3):162–164.

Ernst, C. H., and R. W. Barbour. 1972. *Turtles of the United States.* Lexington: University Press of Kentucky.

Etheridge, R. E. 1952. "The Warty Gecko, *Hemidactylus turcicus turcicus* (Linnaeus), in New Orleans, Louisiana." *Copeia* 1952(1):47–48.

Everitt, C. T. 1971. "Courtship and Mating of *Eumeces multivirgatus* (Scincidae)." *J. Herp.* 5(3–4):189–190.

———. 1974. "Distribution: *Phrynosoma modestum.*" *Herp. Rev.* 5(4):108.

Falko, J. 1973. "The Texas Banded Gecko." *Bull. Canad. Amp. Rep. Conserv. Soc.* 11(2):4–5.

Ferguson, G. W., and T. Brockman. 1980. "Geographic Differences of Growth Rate of *Sceloporus* Lizards (Sauria: Iguanidae)." *Copeia* 1980(2):259–264.

Ferguson, G. W., K. L. Brown, and V. G. DeMarco. 1982. "Selective Basis for the Evolution of Variable Egg and Hatchling Size in Some Iguanid Lizards." *Herpetologica* 38(1):178–188.

Fichter, L. S. 1969. "Geographical Distribution and Osteological Variation in Fossil and Recent Specimens of Two Species of *Kinosternon* (Testudines)." *J. Herp.* 3(3–4):113–119.

Fitch, H. S. 1955. "Habits and Adaptations of the Great Plains Skink (*Eumeces obsoletus*).' *Ecol. Monographs* 25(1):59–83.

———. 1956. "An Ecological Study of the Collared Lizard (*Crotaphytus collaris*)." *Univ. Kansas Publ. Mus. Nat. Hist.* 8(3):213–274.

———. 1958. "Natural History of the Six-lined Racerunner (*Cnemidophorus sexlineatus*)." *Univ. Kansas Publ. Mus. Nat. Hist.* 11(2):11–62.

———. 1967. "Ecological Studies of Lizards on the University of Kansas Natural History Reservation." Pp. 30–44 in *Lizard Ecology: A Symposium,* edited by W. W. Milstead. Missouri: University of Missouri Press.

———. 1970. "Reproductive Cycles of Lizards and Snakes." *Univ. Kansas Mus. Nat. Hist. Misc. Publ.* No. 52:1–247.

————. 1978. "Sexual Size Differences in the Genus *Sceloporus*." *Univ. Kansas Bull.* 51(13):441–461.

————. 1981. "Sexual Size Differences in Reptiles." *Univ. Kansas Mus. Nat. Hist. Misc. Publ.* No. 70:1–73.

————. 1985. "Variation in Clutch and Litter Size in New World Reptiles." *Univ. Kansas Mus. Nat. Hist. Misc. Publ.* No. 76:1–70.

————. 1989. "A Field Study of the Slender Glass Lizard, *Ophisaurus attenuatus*, in Northeastern Kansas." *Occ. Papers Univ. Kansas Mus. Nat. Hist.* No. 125:1–50.

Fitch, H. S., and H. W. Greene. 1965. "Breeding Cycle in the Ground Skink, *Lygosoma laterale*." *Univ. Kansas. Mus. Nat. Hist.* 15(11):565–575.

Fitch, H. S., and D. M. Hillis. 1984. "The *Anolis* Dewlap: Interspecific Variability and Morphological Associations with Habitat." *Copeia* 1984(2):315–323.

Fitch, H. S., and W. W. Tanner. 1951. "Remarks Concerning the Systematics of the Collared Lizard (*Crotaphytus collaris*), with a Description of a New Subspecies." *Trans. Kansas Acad. Sci.* 54(4):548–559.

Flickinger, E. L., and B. M. Mulhern. 1980. "Aldrin Persists in Yellow Mud Turtle." *Herp. Rev.* 11(2):29–30.

Flury, A. 1949. "*Gerrhonotus liocephalus infernalis* Baird in Texas." *Herpetologica* 5(3):65–67.

Fouquette, M. J., Jr., and H. L. Lindsay, Jr. 1955. "An Ecological Survey of Reptiles in Parts of Northwestern Texas." *Texas J. Sci.* 7(4):402–421.

Fox, W., and H. C. Dessauer. 1958. "Growth Rates in Captive Male Green Anoles." *Herpetologica* 14:196–197.

Frierson, L. S., Jr. 1927. "*Phrynosoma cornutum* (Harlan) in Louisiana." *Copeia* 1927(165):114.

Galbraith, D. A., and R. J. Brooks. 1987. "Addition of Annual Growth Lines in Adult Snapping Turtles *Chelydra serpentina*." *J. Herp.* 21(4):359–363.

Gannon, M. R. 1987. "New Western Distributional Record of *Terrapene carolina triunguis*." *Texas J. Sci.* 39(3):293.

Garrett, J. M. and D. G. Barker. 1987. *A Field Guide to Reptiles and Amphibians.* Austin: Texas Monthly Press.

Garriott, J. 1978. "Observations on the Mediterranean Gecko (*Hemidactylus turcicus*)." *Occ. Papers Dallas Herp. Soc.* 1:11–12.

Gehrmann, W. H., and C. C. Carpenter. 1973. "Evidence for a Central Cholinoceptive Component in Despotic Behavior in the Male Collared Lizard, *Crotaphytus collaris*." *Proc. Okla. Acad. Sci.* 53:38–40.

George, J. L., and W. H. Stickel. 1949. "Wildlife Effects of DDT Dust Used for Tick Control on a Texas Prairie." *Amer Midl. Nat.* 42(1):228–237.

Gibbons, J. W. 1983. "Reproductive Characteristics and Ecology of the Mud

148

Turtle, *Kinosternon subrubrum* (Lacepede)." *Herpetologica* 39(3):254–271.

Gibbons, J. W., and D. H. Nelson. 1978. "The Evolutionary Significance of Delayed Emergence from the Nest by Hatchling Turtles." *Evolution* 32:297–303.

Gibbons, J. W., and R. D. Semlitsch. 1982. "Survivorship and Longevity of Long-Lived Vertebrate Species. How Long Do Turtles Live?" *J. Amin. Ecol.* 51:523–527.

Gibbons, J. W., J. L. Greene, and K. K. Patterson. 1982. "Variation in Reproductive Characteristics of Aquatic Turtles." *Copeia* 1982(4):776–784.

Gibbons, J. W., R. D. Semlitsch, J. L. Greene, and J. P. Schubauer. 1981. "Variation in Age and Size at Maturity of the Slider Turtle (*Pseudemys scripta*)." *Amer. Nat.* 117:841–845.

Gibbons, J. W., G. W. Keaton, J. P. Schubauer, J. L. Greene, D. H. Bennett, J. A. McAuliffe, and R. R. Sharitz. 1979. "Unusual Population Size Structure in Freshwater Turtles on Barrier Islands." *Georgia J. Sci.* 37:155–159.

Gilboa, I., and H. G. Dowling. 1972. "A Bibliography on the Longevity of Amphibians and Reptiles." *Publ. Herpetol.* (3):1–6.

Gillette, D. D. 1974. "A Proposed Revision of the Evolutionary History of *Terrapene carolina triunguis*." *Copeia* 1974(2):537–539.

Goff, M. L., and F. W. Judd. 1981. "The First Record of a Chigger from the Texas Tortoise, *Gopherus berlandieri*." *Southwest Nat.* 26(1):83–84.

Goin, C. J., O. B. Goin, and G. R. Zug. 1978. *Introduction to Herpetology.* 3d ed. San Francisco: W. H. Freeman and Co.

Good, D. A. 1987. "A Phylogenetic Analysis of Cranial Osteology in the Gerrhonotine Lizards." *J. Herp.* 21(4):285–297.

———. 1987. "An Allozyme Analysis of Anguid Subfamilial Relationships (Lacertilia: Anguidae)." *Copeia* 1987(3):696–701.

Gordon, R. E. 1956. "The Biology and Biodemography of *Anolis carolinensis* Voigt." Ph.D. dissertation, Tulane University.

———. 1960. "The Influence of Moisture on Variation in the Eggs and Hatchlings of *Anolis c. carolinensis* Voigt." *Nat. Hist. Misc.* No. 173, 6 pp.

Gotch, A. F. 1986. *Reptiles — Their Latin Names Explained.* New York: Blandford Press.

Grant, C. 1936. "The Southwestern Desert Tortoise, *Gopherus agassizii*." *Zoologica* 21(19):225–229.

———. 1960. "Differentiation of the Southwestern Tortoises (Genus *Gopherus*), with Notes on Their Habits." *Trans. San Diego Soc. Nat. Hist.* 12(27):441–448.

Greenberg, B. 1943. "Social Behavior of the Western Banded Gecko, *Coleonyx variegatus* Baird." *Physiol. Zool.* 16:110–122.

Greenberg, B., and G. K. Noble. 1944. "Social Behavior of the American

149

Chameleon (*Anolis carolinensis* Voigt)." *Physiol. Zool.* 1944. 17:392–439.

Greenberg, N., and P. D. MacLean. 1978. *Behavior and Neurology of Lizards*. U.S. Dept. Health, Educ., and Welfare.

Greene, H. W. 1969. "Fat Storage in Females of an Introduced Lizard, *Hemidactylus turcicus*, from Texas." *Texas J. Sci.* 21(2):233–235.

Green, H. W., and B. E. Dial. 1966. "Brooding Behavior by Female Texas Alligator Lizards." *Herpetologica* 22(4):303.

Guidry, E. V. 1953. "Herpetological Notes from Southeastern Texas." *Herpetologica* 9(1):49–56.

Gunter, G. 1945. "The Northern Range of Berlandier's Tortoise." *Copeia* 1945(3):175.

Guttman, S. I. 1971. "An Electrophoretic Analysis of the Hemoglobins of Old and New World Lizards." *J. Herp.* 5(1–2):11–16.

Hallowell, E. 1856. "Note on the Collection of Reptiles from the Neighborhood of San Antonio, Texas, Recently Presented to the Academy of Natural Sciences by Dr. A. Heerman." *Proc. Acad. Nat. Sci. Philadelphia* 8:306–310.

Hambrick, P. S. 1975. "New County Records and Range Extensions of Texas Amphibians and Reptiles." *Herp. Rev.* 6(3):79–80.

————. 1976. "Additions to the Texas Herpetofauna, with Notes on Peripheral Range Extensions and New Records of Texas Amphibians and Reptiles." *Texas J. Sci.* 27(2):291–299.

Hamilton, R. D. 1944. "Notes on Mating and Migration in Berlandier's Turtle." *Copeia* 1944(1):62.

Hamlett, G. W. D. 1952. "Notes on Breeding and Reproduction in the Lizard *Anolis carolinensis*." *Copeia* 1952(3):183–185.

Hampton, N. 1976. "Annotated Checklist of the Amphibians and Reptiles of Travis County, Texas." Pp. 84–101 in *A Bird Finding and Naturalists' Guide for the Austin, Texas, Area*, edited by E. A. Kutac and S. C. Caran. Austin, Texas: Oasis Press.

Harper, F. 1932. "A New Texas Subspecies of the Lizard Genus *Holbrookia*." *Proc. Biol. Soc. Wash.* 45:15–18.

Hart, D. R. 1983. "Dietary and Habitat Shift with Size of Red-eared Turtles (*Pseudemys scripta*) in a Southern Louisiana Population." *Herpetologica* 39(3):285–290.

Hartweg, N. 1939. "Further Notes on the *Pseudemys scripta* Complex." *Copeia* 1939(1):55.

Haynes, D., and R. R. McKown. 1974. "A New Species of Map Turtle (Genus *Graptemys*) from the Guadalupe River System in Texas." *Tulane Stud. Zool. Bot.* 18(4):143–152.

Hendricks, A. C., J. T. Wyatt, and D. E. Henley. 1971. "Infestation of a Texas Red-eared Turtle by Leeches." *Texas J. Sci.* 22(2–3):247.

Hensley, M. 1968. "Another Albino Lizard, *Sceloporus undulatus hyacinthinus*

(Green)." *J. Herp.* 1(1–4):92–93.

Herald, E. S. 1949. "Effects of DDT-Oil Solutions upon Amphibians and Reptiles." *Herpetologica* 5:117–120.

Hewatt, W. G. 1937. "Courting and Egg-Laying Habits of *Phrynosoma cornutum*." *Copeia* 1937(4):234.

Hildebrand, M. 1982. *Analysis of Vertebrate Structure.* 2nd ed. New York: John Wiley and Sons.

Hoddenbach, G. A. 1966. "Reproduction in Western Texas *Cnemidophorus sexlineatus* (Sauria: Teiidae)." *Copeia* 1966(1):110–113.

Hoff, G. L., and D. O. Trainer. 1973. "Arboviruses in Reptiles: Isolation of a Bunyamwera Group Virus from a Naturally Infected Turtle." *J. Herp.* 7(2):55–62.

Hoffmann, C. H., and J. P. Linduska. 1949. "Some Considerations of the Biological Effects of DDT." *Sci. Monthly* 69:104–114.

Holman, J. A. 1969. "The Pleistocene Amphibians and Reptiles of Texas." *Publ. Michigan St. Mus. Biol. Ser.* 4(5):163–192.

Houseal, T. W., and J. L. Carr. 1983. "Notes on the Reproduction of *Kinosternon subrubrum* (Testudines: Kinosternidae) in East Texas." *Southwest. Nat.* 28(2):237–239.

Houseal, T. W., J. W. Bickham, and M. D. Springer. 1982. "Geographic Variation in the Yellow Mud Turtle, *Kinosternon flavescens.*" *Copeia* 1982(3):567–580.

Hoyt, J. S. Y. 1941. "High Speed Attained by *Cnemidophorus sexlineatus.*" *Copeia* 1941 (3):180.

Huey, R. B., E. R. Pianka, and T. W. Schoener. 1983. *Lizard Ecology: Studies of a Model Organism.* Massachusetts: Harvard University Press.

Hunsaker, D. II. 1959. "Stomach Contents of the American Egret, *Casmerodius albus,* in Travis County, Texas." *Texas J. Sci.* 11(4):454.

Hutchison, V. H., A. Vinegar, and R. J. Kosh. 1966. "Critical Thermal Maxima in Turtles." *Herpetologica* 22:32–41.

Iverson, J. B. 1977. "Reproduction in Freshwater and Terrestrial Turtles of North Florida." *Herpetologica* 33:205–212.

––––––. 1978. "Distributional Problems of the Genus *Kinosternon* in the American Southwest." *Copeia* 1978(3):476–479.

––––––. 1979. "A Taxonomic Reappraisal of the Yellow Mud Turtle, *Kinosternon flavescens* (Testudines: Kinosternidae)." *Copeia* 1979(2):212–215.

––––––. 1985. "Geographic Variation in Sexual Dimorphism in the Mud Turtle *Kinosternon hirtipes.*" *Copeia* 1985(2):388–393.

Jameson, D. L., and A. G. Flury. "The Reptiles and Amphibians of the Sierra Vieja Range of Southwestern Texas." *Texas J. Sci.* 1(2):54–79.

Johnson, C. 1960. "Reproductive Cycle in Females of the Greater Earless Lizard, *Holbrookia texana.*" *Copeia* 1960(4):297–300.

Jones, S. M., and G. W. Ferguson. 1980. "The Effect of Paint Marking on Mortality in a Texas Population of *Sceloporus undulatus.*" *Copeia*

151

1980(4):850–854.

Judd, F. W. 1974. "The Ecology of the Keeled Earless Lizard, *Holbrookia propinqua.*" *Diss. Abstr. Int.* B35(1):599–600.

———. 1974. "Intraspecific Variation in Blood Properties of the Keeled Earless Lizard, *Holbrookia propinqua.*" *Herpetologica* 30(1):99–102.

———. 1975. "Activity and Thermal Ecology of the Keeled Earless Lizard, *Holbrookia propinqua.*" *Herpetologica* 31(2):137–150.

———. 1976. "Demography of a Barrier Island Population of the Keeled Earless Lizard, *Holbrookia propinqua.*" *Occ. Papers Mus. Texas Tech. Univ.* No. 44:1–45.

———. 1976. "Food and Feeding behavior of the Keeled Earless Lizard, *Holbrookia propinqua.*" *Southwest. Nat.* 21(1):17–26.

———. 1982. "Notes on Longevity of *Gopherus berlandieri* (Testudinidae)." *Southwest Nat.* 27(2):230–232.

Judd, F. W., and F. L. Rose. 1983. "Population Structure, Density and Movements of the Texas Tortoise *Gopherus berlandieri.*" *Southwest. Nat.* 28(4):387–398.

Judd, F. W., and J. C. McQueen. 1980. "Incubation, Hatching, and Growth of Tortoise, *Gopherus berlandieri.*" *J. Herp.* 14(4):377–380.

Judd, F. W., and R. K. Ross. 1978. "Year-to-Year Variation in Clutch Size of Island and Mainland Populations of *Holbrookia propinqua* (Reptilia, Lacertilia, Iguanidae)." *J. Herp.* 12(2):203–207.

Judd, F. W., F. L. Rose, and J. C. McQueen. 1980. "Population Structure, Size Relationships, and Growth of the Texas Tortoise, *Gopherus berlandieri.*" P. 186 (abstract) in *Desert Tortoise Council Proc. 1979 Symposium,* edited by E. St. Amant, S. Allan, and R. Kirwan.

Karges, J. P. 1978. "Texas Amphibians and Reptiles: Some New Distributional Records, Part I." *Herp. Rev.* 9(4):143–145.

———. 1979. "Texas Amphibians and Reptiles: Some New Distributional Records, Part II." *Herp. Rev.* 10(4):119–121.

———. 1981. "Texas Amphibians and Reptiles: Some New Distributional Records, Part III." *Herp. Rev.* 12(2):68–69.

———. 1982. "Texas Amphibians and Reptiles: Some New Distributional Records, Part IV." *Herp. Rev.* 13(1):27.

Kennedy, J. P. 1956. "Food Habits of the Rusty Lizard, *Sceloporus olivaceus* Smith." *Texas J. Sci.* 8(3):328–349.

———. 1959. "Sleeping Habits of the Eastern Fence Lizard, *Sceloporus undulatus hyacinthinus* (Sauria, Iguanidae)." *Southwest Nat.* 3:90–93.

Keown, G. 1972. "Geographical Distribution, *Hemidactylus turcicus turcicus.*" *Herp. Rev.* 4(5):170.

Killebrew, F. G. 1975. "Mitotic Chromosomes of Turtles. III. The Kinosternidae." *Herpetologica* 31(4):398–403.

Klein, T., Jr. 1951. "A New Method of Collecting *Holbrookia texana.*" *Herpetologica* 7:200.

Kluge, A. G. 1962. "Comparative Osteology of the Eublepharid Lizard Genus *Coleonyx* Gray." *J. Morph.* 110(3):299–332.

———. 1975. "Phylogenetic Relationships and Evolutionary Trends in the Eublepharine Lizard Genus *Coleonyx*." *Copeia* 1975(1):24–25.

Knowlton, G. F. 1948. "Some Insect Food of *Sceloporus poinsettii* B&G." *Herpetologica* 4:151–152.

Kofron, C. P., and A. A. Schreiber. 1985. "Ecology of Two Endangered Aquatic Turtles in Missouri: *Kinosternon flavescens* and *Emydoidea blandingii*." *J. Herp.* 19(1):27–40.

———. 1987. "Observations on Aquatic Turtles in a Northeastern Missouri Marsh." *Southwest. Nat.* 32(4):517–521.

Lamb, T., J. C. Avise, and J. W. Gibbons. 1989. "Phylogeographic Patterns in Mitochondrial DNA of the Desert Tortoise (*Xerobates agassizi*), and Evolutionary Relationships Among the North American Gopher Tortoises." *Evolution* 43(1):76–87.

Lambert, S. 1985. "Blood Ejection Frequency by *Phrynosoma cornutum* (Iguanidae)." *Southwest. Nat.* 30(4):616–617.

Lardie, R. L. 1963. "A Length Record for *Trionyx spinifer emoryi* (Agassiz)." *Herpetologica* 19(2):150.

———. 1964. "Pugnacious Behavior in the Softshell *Trionyx spinifer pallidus* and Implications of Territoriality. *Herpetologica* 20(4):281–284.

———. 1975. "Courtship and Mating Behavior in the Yellow Mud Turtle, *Kinosternon flavescens flavescens*." *J. Herp.* 9(2):223–227.

———. 1975. "Observations on Reproduction in *Kinosternon*." *J. Herp.* 9(2):260–264.

———. 1979. "Eggs and Young of the Plain's Yellow Mud Turtle." *Bull. Oklahoma Herp. Soc.* 4(2–3):24–30.

———. 1980. "Winter Activity of *Chrysemys scripta elegans* (Wied-Neuwied) in North Central Texas." *Bull. Oklahoma Herp. Soc.* 4(4):72–76.

Lee, S. H. 1955. "The Mode of Egg Dispersal in *Physaloptera phrynosoma* Ortlepp (Nematoda: Spiruroidea), A Gastric Nematode of Texas Horned Toads, *Phrynosoma cornutum*." *J. Parasit.* 41(1):70–74.

Legler, J. M. 1959. "A New Tortoise, Genus *Gopherus*, from North-central Mexico." *Univ. Kansas Publ. Mus. Nat. Hist. Publ.* 11(5):335–343.

———. 1960. "Natural History of the Ornate Box Turtle, *Terrapene ornata ornata* Agassiz." *Univ. Kansas Publ. Mus. Nat. Hist. Publ.* 11:527–669.

———. 1960. "A New Subspecies of Slider Turtle (*Pseudemys scripta*) from Coahuila, Mexico." *Univ. Kansas Publ. Mus. Nat. Hist.* 13(3):73–84.

Lewis, M. R. 1974. "Recent County Records and Range Extensions from Southcentral Texas." *Herp. Rev.* 5(1):21.

Lewis, T. H. 1951. "The Biology of *Leiolopisma laterale* (Say)." *Amer. Midl. Nat.* 45(1):232–240.

Licht, P. 1967. "Environmental Control of Annual Testicular Cycles in the Lizard *Anolis carolinensis*." *J. Exp. Zool.* 165:505–516.

153

————. 1973. "Influence of Temperature and Photoperiod on the Annual Ovarian Cycle in the Lizard *Anolis carolinensis*." *Copeia* 1973:465–472.

Lieb, C. S. 1985. "Systematics and Distribution of the Skinks Allied to *Eumeces tetragrammus* (Sauria: Scincidae)." *Nat. Hist. Mus. Los Angeles County Contributions in Science* No. 357, pp. 1–19.

Long, D. R. 1986. "Clutch Formation in the Turtle, *Kinosternon flavescens* (Testudines: Kinosternidae)." *Southwest Nat.* 31(1):1–8.

————. 1986. "Lipid Content and Delayed Emergence of Hatchling Yellow Mud Turtles." *Southwest Nat.* 31(2):244–246.

MacFarland, W. N., F. H. Pough, T. J. Cade, and J. B. Heiser. 1985. *Vertebrate Life*. 2nd ed. New York: Macmillan Pub. Co.

Mahmoud, I. Y. 1967. "Courtship Behavior and Sexual Maturity in Four Species of Kinosternid Turtles." *Copeia* 1967(2):314–319.

————. 1968. "Feeding Behavior in Kinosternid Turtles." *Herpetologica* 24(4):300–305.

————. 1969. "Comparative Ecology of the Kinosternid Turtles of Oklahoma." *Southwest Nat.* 14:31–66.

Mahmoud, I. Y. and J. Klicka. 1972. "Seasonal Gonadal Changes in Kinosternid Turtles." *J. Herp.* 6(3–4):183–189.

Marcus, L. C. 1981. *Veterinary Biology and Medicine of Captive Amphibians and Reptiles*. Philadelphia: Lea and Febiger.

Mares, M. A. 1971. "Coprophagy in the Texas Tortoise. *Gopherus berlandieri*." *Texas J. Sci.* 23(2):300.

Marion, K. R., J. R. Bizer, and O. J. Sexton. 1979. "A Between-Clutch Comparison of Hatchling Weights in the Lizard *Sceloporus undulatus* (Reptilia: Squamata: Lacertilia)." *Herpetologica* 35(2):111–114.

Marr, J. C. 1944. "Notes on Amphibians and Reptiles from the Central United States." *Amer. Midl. Nat.* 32(2):478–490.

Martin, R. F. 1973. "Reproduction in the Tree Lizard (*Urosaurus ornatus*) in Central Texas: Drought Conditions." *Herpetologica* 29(1):27–32.

————. 1977. "Variation in Reproductive Productivity of Range Margin Tree Lizards (*Urosaurus ornatus*)." *Copeia* 1977(1):83–92.

————. 1978. "Clutch Weight/Total Body Weight Ratios of Lizards (Reptilia, Lacertilia, Iguanidae): Preservative Induced Variation." *J. Herp.* 12(2):248–251.

Mather, C. M. 1970. "Some Aspects of the Life History of the Ground Skink, *Lygosoma laterale*." *Texas J. Sci.* 21(4):429–438.

————. 1976. "Comparative Ecology of Two Lizards (*Sceloporus variabilis* and *Sceloporus undulatus*) in an Area of Sympatry." *Diss. Abstr. Int.* B37(8): 3756.

————. 1978. "A Case of Limb Regeneration in *Sceloporus variabilis* (Reptilia, Lacertilia, Iguanidae)." *J. Herp.* 12(2):263.

Mather, C. M., and J. R. Dixon. 1976. "Geographic Records of Some South Texas Amphibians and Reptiles." *Herp. Rev.* 7(3):127.

154

Mathewson, J. J. 1979. "Enterobacteriaceae Isolated from Iguanid Lizards of West-Central Texas." *Appl. Environ. Microbiol.* 38:402–405.

McAllister, C. T. 1982. "Geographic Distribution, *Chrysemys concinna.*" *Herp. Rev.* 13(3):80.

―――. 1983. "Life History Notes. *Crotaphytus collaris collaris* (Eastern Collared Lizard). Hibernacula." *Herp. Rev.* 14(3):73–74.

―――. 1984. "Life History Notes. *Crotaphytus collaris collaris* (Eastern Collared Lizard). Reproduction." *Herp. Rev.* 15(2):48.

―――. 1985. "Food Habits and Feeding Behavior of *Crotaphytus collaris collaris* (Iguanidae) from Arkansas and Missouri." *Southwest. Nat.* 30(4):597–619.

―――. 1987. "Ingestion of Spinose Ear Ticks *Otobius megnini* (Acari: Argasidae) by a Texas Spotted Whiptail *Cnemidophorus gularis gularis* (Sauria: Teiidae)." *Southwest. Nat.* 32(4):511–512.

McAllister, C. T., and S. P. Tabor. 1985. "Geographic Distribution. *Cnemidophorus sexlineatus viridis.*" *Herp. Rev.* 16(3):83.

McAllister, C. T., and S. E. Trauth. 1982. "An Instance of the Eastern Collared Lizard, *Crotaphytus collaris collaris* (Sauria: Iguanidae) Feeding on *Sigmodon hispidus* (Rodentia: Cricetidae)." *Southwest. Nat.* 27(3):358–359.

―――. 1985. "Endoparasites of *Crotaphytus collaris collaris* (Sauria: Iguanidae) from Arkansas." *Southwest. Nat.* 30(3):363–370.

McAllister, C. T., and R. Ward. 1986. "More Distributional Records of Amphibians and Reptiles from Texas." *Herp. Rev.* 17(1):28–30.

―――. 1986. "New Distributional Records of Texas Herpetofauna." *Texas J. Sci.* 38(1):65–69.

McAllister, C. T., and M. C. Wooten. 1981. "Geographic Distribution, *Cnemidophorus gularis.*" *Herp. Rev.* 12(3):84.

McAllister, C. T., R. Ward, and J. R. Glidewell. 1983. "New Distributional Records for Selected Amphibians and Reptiles of Texas." *Herp. Rev.* 14(2):52–53.

McClure, W. L. 1967. "*Terrapene carolina triunguis* from the Late Pleistocene of Southeast Texas." *Herpetologica* 23(4):321–322.

McConkey, E. H. 1954. "A Systematic Study of the North American Lizards of the Genus *Ophisaurus.*" *Amer. Midl. Nat.* 51(1):133–169.

McCuller, R. E., and G. G. Raun. 1971. "Notes on the Distribution of Some Reptiles and Amphibians in Northeastern Texas." *Southwest. Nat.* 16(2):220.

McKee, C. R., and S. Martinez, Jr. 1981. "An Endoparasite of *Holbrookia propinqua propinqua* (Iguanidae)." *Southwest. Nat.* 26(1):75–76.

McKinney, C. O., and R. E. Ballinger. 1966. "Snake Predators of Lizards in Western Texas." *Southwest Nat.* 11(3):410–412.

Mecham, J. S. 1959. "Some Pleistocene Amphibians and Reptiles from Friesenhahn Cave, Texas." *Southwest. Nat.* 3:17–27.

Merkord, G. W. 1975. "Range Extensions and New County Records of Some

Texas Amphibians and Reptiles." *Herp. Rev.* 6(3):79.

Metcalf, A. L., and E. L. Metcalf. 1985. "Longevity in Some Ornate Box Turtles (*Terrapene ornata ornata*)." *J. Herp.* 19(1):157–158.

Metcalf, E. L., and A. L. Metcalf. 1970. "Observations on ornate box turtles (*Terrapene ornata ornata* Agassiz)." *Trans. Kansas Acad. Sci.* 73:95–117.

———. 1979. "Mortality in Hibernating Ornate Box Turtles, *Terrapene ornata.*" *Herpetologica* 35(1):93–96.

Meylan, P. A. 1987. "The Phylogenetic Relationships of Soft-shelled Turtles (Family Trionychidae)." *Bull. Amer. Mus. Nat. Hist.* 186(1):1–101.

Michael, E. D., 1969. "A Longevity Record for a Non-captive *Anolis carolinensis.*" *Herpetologica* 25(4):318.

———. 1972. "Growth Rates in *Anolis carolinenesis.*" *Copeia* 1972(3):575–577.

Michael, E. D., and T. F. Bailey. 1973. "Hibernation Sites of *Anolis carolinensis* and *Sceloporus undulatus.*" *Texas J. Sci.* 24(3):351–353.

Miller, D. 1983. "Creatures of the Desert — The Texas Alligator Lizard." *Chihuahuan Desert Discovery* 6:3.

Milne, L. J. 1938. "Mating of *Phrynosoma cornutum.*" *Copeia* 1938(4):200.

Milstead, W. W. 1953. "Ecological Distribution of the Lizards of La Mota Mountain Region of Trans-Pecos Texas." *Texas J. Sci.* 5(4):403–415.

———. 1956. "Fossil turtles of Friesehahn Cave, Texas with the Description of a New Species *Testudo.*" *Copeia* 1956(3):162–171.

———. 1957. "Observations on the Natural History of Four Species of Whiptail Lizard, *Cnemidophorus* (Sauria, Teiidae) in Trans-Pecos Texas." *Southwest Nat.* 2(2–3):105–121.

———. 1957. "Some Aspects of Competition in Natural Populations of Whiptail Lizards (Genus *Cnemidophorus*)." *Texas J. Sci.* 9(4):410–447.

———. 1958. "A List of the Arthropods Found in the Stomachs of Whiptail Lizards from Four Stations in Southwestern Texas." *Texas J. Sci.* 10(4):443–446.

———. 1959. "Drift-Fence Trapping of Lizards on the Black Gap Wildlife Management Area of Southwestern Texas." *Texas J. Sci.* 11(2):150–157.

———. 1960. "Relict Species of the Chihuahuan Desert." *Southwest Nat.* 5(2):75–88.

———. 1960. "Supplementary Notes on the Herpetofauna of the Stockton Plateau." *Texas J. Sci.* 12(3–4):228–231.

———. 1961. "Observations of the Activities of Small Animals (Reptilia and Mammalia) on a Quadrat in Southwest Texas." *Amer. Midl. Nat.* 65(1):127–138.

———. 1965. *Lizard Ecology — A Symposium.* Missouri: University of Missouri Press.

———. 1965. "Notes on the Identities of Some Poorly Known Fossils of Box Turtles (*Terrapene*)." *Copeia* 1965(4):513–514.

————. 1970. "Late Summer Behavior of the Lizards *Sceloporus merriami* and *Urosaurus ornatus* in the Field." *Herpetologica* 26(3):343–354.

Milstead, W. W., and D. W. Tinkle. 1969. "Interrelationships of Feeding Habits in a Population of Lizards in Southwestern Texas." *Amer. Midl. Nat.* 81(2):491–499.

Milstead, W. W., J. S. Mecham, and H. McClintock. 1950. "The Amphibians and Reptiles of the Stockton Plateau in Northern Terrell County, Texas." *Texas J. Sci.* 2(4):543–562.

Minton, S. A., Jr., 1959. "Observations on Amphibians and Reptiles of the Big Bend Region of Texas." *Southwest. Nat.* 3:28–54.

Mitchell, J. C. 1979. "The Concept of Phenology and Its Application to the Study of Amphibian and Reptile Life Histories." *Herp. Rev.* 10(2):51–54.

Mittleman, M. B. 1942. "A Summary of the Iguanid Genus *Urosaurus.*" *Bull. Mus. Comp. Zool.* 91(2):103–181.

————. 1947. "Notes on *Gopherus berlandieri* (Agassiz)." *Copeia* 1947(3):211.

Moll, E. O., and K. L. Williams. 1963. "The Musk Turtle *Sternothaerus odoratus* from Mexico." *Copeia* 1963(1):157.

Montanucci, R. R. 1974. "Convergence, Polymorphism or Introgressive Hybridization? An Analysis of Interaction Between *Crotaphytus collaris* and *C. reticulatus* (Sauria: Iguanidae)." *Copeia* 1974(1):87–101.

Montanucci, R. R., R. W. Axtell, and H. C. Dessauer. 1975. "Evolutionary Divergence Among Collared Lizards (*Crotaphytus*) with Comments on the Status of *Gambelia.*" *Herpetologica* 31(3):336–347.

Morreale, S. J., J. W. Gibbons, and J. D. Congdon. 1984. "Significance of Activity and Movement in the Yellow-bellied Slider Turtle (*Pseudemys scripta*)." *Canad. J. Zool.* 62:1038–1042.

Morris, K. A., G. C. Packard, T. J. Boardman, G. L. Paukstis, and M. J. Packard. 1983. "Effect of the Hydric Environment on Growth of Embryonic Snapping Turtles (*Chelydra serpentina*)." *Herpetologica* 39(3):272–285.

Morrison, E. O. 1961. "A New Locality Record for the Warty Gecko." *Texas J. Sci.* 13(3):357.

Mount, R. H. 1975. *The Reptiles and Amphibians of Alabama.* Alabama: Auburn Printing Co.

Mueller, A. J. 1985. "Vertebrate Use of Nontidal Wetlands of Galveston Island, Texas." *Texas J. Sci.* 37(2–3):215–225.

Mulaik, S. 1935. "Tail Regeneration in *Coleonyx brevis* Stejneger." *Copeia* 1935(3):155–156.

Murphy, J. C. 1976. "The Natural History of the Box Turtle." *Bull. Chicago Herp. Soc.* 11(1–4):2–45.

Myers, S. 1982. "Geographic Distribution, *Chrysemys concinna.*" *Herp. Rev.*

157

13(1):24.

―――. 1983. "Geographic Distribution, *Chrysemys scripta elegans.*" *Herp. Rev.* 14(3):83.

―――. 1983. "Geographic Distribution, *Leiolopisma laterale.*" *Herp. Rev.* 14(3):84.

Neck, R. W. 1977. "Cutaneous Myiasis in *Gopherus berlandieri* (Reptilia, Testudines, Testudinidae)." *J. Herp.* 11(1):96–98.

―――. 1980. "Geographical Distribution, *Terrapene o. ornata.*" *Herp. Rev.* 11(2):38.

―――. 1982. "Geographical Distribution, *Cnemidophorus gularis gularis.*" *Herp. Rev.* 13(3):80.

Neck, R. W., D. H. Riskind, and K. Peterson. 1979. "Geographical Distribution, *Gerrhonotus liocephalis infernalis.*" *Herp. Rev.* 10(4):118.

Newcomb, W. W. 1961. *The Indians of Texas from Prehistoric to Modern Times.* Austin, Texas: University of Texas Press.

Norris, K. S., and C. H. Lowe. 1964. "An Analysis of Background Color-Matching in Amphibians and Reptiles." *Ecology* 45(3):565–580.

O'Brien, G. P., H. K. Smith, and J. R. Meyer. 1965. "An Activity Study of a Radioisotope-Tagged Lizard, *Sceloporus undulatus hyacinthinus* (Sauria: Iguanidae)." *Southwest. Nat.* 10(3):179–187.

Odum, R. A. 1985. "Life History Notes, *Pseudemys scripta elegans* Deformity." *Herp. Rev.* 16(4):113.

Ohlendorf, S. M., J. M. Bigelow, and M. M. Standifer. 1980. *Journey to Mexico During the Years 1826–1834.* 2 vols. Austin: Texas State Historical Association.

Olson, R. E. 1959. "Notes on Some Texas Herptiles." *Herpetologica* 15:48.

―――. 1967. "Peripheral Range Extensions and Some New Records of Texas Amphibians and Reptiles." *Texas J. Sci.* 19(1):99–106.

―――. 1976. "Weight Regimes in the Tortoise *Gopherus berlandieri.*" *Texas J. Sci.* 17(2):321–323.

―――. 1987. "Evaporative Water Loss in the Tortoise *Gopherus berlandieri* in Ambient Temperature Regimes." *Bull. Maryland Herp. Soc.* 23(3):93–100.

Orleb, E. 1951. "*Thamnophis sirtalis sirtalis* eats *Anolis carolinensis.*" *Herpetologica* 7(2):76.

Packard, G. C., C. R. Tracy, and J. J. Roth. 1977. "The Physiological Ecology of Reptilian Eggs and Embryos, and the Evolution of Viviparity within the Class Reptilia." *Biol. Rev.* 52:71–105.

Parker, J. W. 1982. "Opportunistic Feeding by an Ornate Box Turtle Under the Nest of a Mississippi Kite." *Southwest. Nat.* 27(3):365.

Parker, W. S. 1973. "Notes on Reproduction of Some Lizards from Arizona, New Mexico, Texas, and Utah." *Herpetologica* 29(3):258–264.

―――. 1984. "Immigration and Dispersal of Slider Turtles *Pseudemys scripta* in Mississippi Farm Ponds." *Amer. Midl. Nat.* 112(2):280–293.

Parmenter, R. R. 1980. "Effects of Food Availability and Water Temperature on the Feeding Ecology of Pond Sliders (*Chrysemys s. scripta*)." *Copeia* 1980(3):503–514.

Parmley, D. 1982. "Food Items of Roadrunners from Palo Pinto County, North Central Texas." *Texas J. Sci.* 34(1):94–95.

Paulissen, M. A. 1987. "Diet of Adult and Juvenile Six-lined Racerunners, *Cnemidophorus sexlineatus* (Sauria: Teiidae)." *Southwest Nat.* 32(3):395–397.

———. 1988. "Ontogenetic and Seasonal Shifts in Microhabitat Use by the Lizard *Cnemidophorus sexlineatus*." *Copeia* 1988(4):1021–1029.

———. 1988. "Ontogenetic Comparison of Body Temperature Selection and Thermal Tolerance of *Cnemidophorus sexlineatus*." *J. Herp.* 22(4):473–476.

Paxson, D. W. 1961. "An Observation of Eggs in a Tortoise Shell." *Herpetologica* 17(4):278–279.

Pence, D. B., and K. W. Selcer. 1988. "Effects of Pentastome Infection on Reproduction in a Southern Texas Population of the Mediterranean Gecko, *Hemidactylus turcicus*." *Copeia* 1988(3):565–572.

Peters, J. A. 1964. *Dictionary of Herpetology*. New York: Hafner Publishing Company.

Pianka, E. R. 1976. "Natural Selection of Optimal Reproductive Tactics." *Amer. Zool.* 16:775–784.

———. 1986. *Ecology and Natural History of Desert Lizards*. New Jersey: Princeton University Press.

Pianka, E. R., and W. S. Parker. 1975. "Ecology of Horned Lizards: A Review with Special Reference to *Phrynosoma platyrhinos*." *Copeia* 1975(1):141–162.

Pietruszka, R. D. 1981. "Use of Scutellation for Distinguishing Sexes in Bisexual Species of *Cnemidophorus*." *Herpetologica* 37(4):244–249.

Pilch, J., Jr. 1981. "Life History Notes, *Chrysemys concinna texana* Morphology." *Herp. Rev.* 12(3):81.

Pope, C. H. 1946. *Turtles of the United States and Canada*. New York: Alfred A. Knopf.

Potter, G. E., and S. O. Brown. 1941. "Color Changes in *Phrynosoma cornutum*." *Proc. Trans. Texas Acad. Sci.* 4(1):7 (abstract).

———. 1941. "Effect of Sex and Gonadotropic Hormones on the Development of the Gonads in *Phrynosoma cornutum* during Reproductive and Non-reproductive Phases." *Trans. Texas Acad. Sci.* 25:55–56.

Potter, G. E., and H. B. Glass. 1931. "A Study of Respiration in Hibernating Horned Lizards, *Phrynosoma cornutum*." *Copeia* 1931(3):128–131.

Price, A. H. 1980. "Geographical Distribution, *Hemidactylus turcicus*." *Herp. Rev.* 11(2):39.

Price, P. W. 1974. "Strategies for Egg Production." *Evolution* 28:76–84.

Pritchard, P. C. H. 1979. *Encyclopedia of Turtles*. New Jersey: T.F.H. Publications, Inc.

Pritchett, A. H. 1903. "Some Experiments in Feeding Lizards with Protectively Colored Insects." *Biol. Bull.* 5:271–287.

Punzo, F. 1974. "An Analysis of the Stomach Contents of the Gecko, *Coleonyx brevis.*" *Copeia* 1974(3):779–780.

———. 1974. "A Qualitative and Quantitative Study of Food Items of the Yellow Mud Turtle, *Kinosternon flavescens* (Agassiz)." *J. Herp.* 8(3):269–271.

———. 1975. "Studies on the Feeding Behavior, Diet, Nesting Habits and Temperature Relationships of *Chelydra serpentina osceola* (Chelonia: Chelydridae)." *J. Herp.* 9(2):207–210.

———. 1976. "Analysis of the pH and Electrolyte Components Found in the Blood Plasma of Several Species of West Texas Reptiles." *J. Herp.* 10(1):49–52.

———. 1982. "Clutch and Egg Size in Several Species of Lizards from the Desert Southwest." *J. Herp.* 16(4):414–417.

———. 1982. "Tail Autotomy and Running Speed in the Lizards *Cophosaurus texanus* and *Uma notata.*" *J. Herp.* 16(3):329–331.

Pyburn, W. F. 1955. "Species Discrimination in Two Sympatric Lizards, *Sceloporus olivaceus* and *S. poinsetti.*" *Texas J. Sci.* 7(2):312–315.

Rakowitz, V. A., R. R. Fleet, and F. L. Rainwater. 1983. "New Distributional Records of Texas Amphibians and Reptiles." *Herp. Rev.* 14(3):85–89.

Ramsey, L. W. 1948. "Hibernation of *Holbrookia texana.*" *Herpetologica* 4(6):223.

———. 1949. "Hibernation, and the Effect of a Flood on *Holbrookia texana.*" *Herpetologica* 5(6):125–126.

———. 1956. "Nesting of Texas Horned Lizards." *Herpetologica* 12(3):239–240.

Ramsey, L. W., and E. T. Donlon. 1949. "The Young of the Lizard *Sceloporus poinsetii.*" *Copeia* 1949(3):229.

Raun, G. G. 1959. "Terrestrial and Aquatic Vertebrates of a Moist, Relict Area in Central Texas." *Texas J. Sci.* 11(2):158–171.

———. 1965. "Western Limits of Distribtuion of the Stinkpot, *Sternothaerus odoratus* in Texas." *Herpetologica* 21(1):69–71.

Raun, G. G., and F. R. Gehlbach. 1972. "Amphibians and Reptiles in Texas." *Dallas Mus. Nat. Hist. Mus. Bull.* 2:1–61.

Reddell, J. R. 1970. "A Checklist of the Cave Fauna of Texas. VI. Additional Records of Vertebrata." *Texas J. Sci.* 22(2–3):139–158.

Reynolds, S. L., and M. E. Seidel. 1983. "Morphological Homogeneity in the Turtle *Sternotherus odoratus* (Kinosternidae) Throughout Its Range." *J. Herp.* 17(2):113–120.

Robinson, C., and J. R. Bider. 1988. "Nesting Synchrony — A Strategy to

Decrease Predation of Snapping Turtle (*Chelydra serpentina*) Nests." *J. Herp.* 22(4):470–473.

Rogers, J. S. 1976. "Species Density and Taxonomic Diversity of Texas Amphibians and Reptiles." *Syst. Zool.* 25(1):26–40.

Rose, B. 1982. "Lizard Home Ranges: Methodology and Functions." *J. Herp.* 16(3):253–269.

Rose, F. L. 1969. "Desiccation Rates and Temperature Relationships of *Terrapene ornata* Following Scute Removal." *Southwest. Nat.* 14(1):67–72.

———. 1980. "Home Range Estimates of *Gopherus berlandieri*." P. 187 (abstract) in *Desert Tortoise Council Proc., 1979 Symposium*, edited by E. St. Amant, S. Allen, and R. Kirwan.

Rose, F. L., and C. D. Barbour. 1968. "Ecology and Reproductive Cycles of the Introduced Gecko, *Hemidactylus turcicus*, in the Southern United States." *Amer. Midl. Nat.* 79(1):159–168.

Rose, F. L., and F. W. Judd. 1975. "Activity and Home Range Size of the Texas Tortoise, *Gopherus berlandieri*, in South Texas." *Herpetologica* 31(4): 448–456.

Rose, F. L., M. T. Scholl, and M. P. Moulton. 1988. "Thermal Preferentia of Berlandier's Tortoise *(Gopherus berlandieri)* and the Ornate Box Turtle *(Terrapene ornata)*." *Southwest. Nat.* 33(3):357–390.

Ross, R. K., and F. W. Judd. 1982. "Comparison of Lipid Cycles of *Holbrookia propinqua* from Padre Island and Mainland Texas." *J. Herp.* 16(1):53–60.

Sabath, M. 1960. "Eggs and Young of Several Reptiles." *Herpetologica* 16(1):72.

Sabath, M., and R. Worthington. 1959. "Eggs and Young of Certain Texas Reptiles." *Herpetologica* 15(1):31–32.

Schall, J. J. 1977. "Thermal Ecology of Five Sympatric Species of *Cnemidophorus* (Sauria:Teiidae)." *Herpetologica* 33(3):261–272.

———. 1978. "Reproductive Strategies in Sympatric Whiptail Lizards *(Cnemidophorus)*: Two Parthenogenetic and Three Bisexual Species." *Copeia* 1978(1):108–116.

Schoener, T. W. 1982. "Intraspecific Variation in Home-Range Size in Some *Anolis* Lizards." *Ecology* 63(3):809–823.

Schrank, G. D., and R. E. Ballinger. 1973. "Male Reproductive Cycles in Two Species of Lizards *(Cophosaurus texanus* and *Cnemidophorus gularis)*." *Herpetologica* 29(3):289–293.

Scribner, K. T., J. E. Evans, S. J. Morreale, M. H. Smith, and J. W. Gibbons. 1986. "Genetic Divergence among Populations of the Yellow-bellied Slider Turtle *(Pseudemys scripta)* Separated by Aquatic and Terrestrial Habitats." *Copeia* 1986(3):691–700.

Scudday, J. F., and J. R. Dixon. 1973. "Diet and Feeding Behavior of Teiid Lizards from Trans-Pecos, Texas." *Southwest. Nat.* 18(3):279–289.

Seidel, M. E., J. B. Iverson, and M. D. Adkins. 1986. "Biochemical Comparisons and Phylogenetic Relationships in the Family Kinosternidae (Testudines)." *Copeia* 1986(2):285–294.

Seidel, M. E., S. L. Reynolds, and R. V. Lucchino. 1981. "Phylogenetic Relationships Among Musk Turtles (Genus *Sternotherus*) and Genic Variation in *Sternotherus odoratus*." *Herpetologica* 37(3):161–165.

Seifert, W. 1978. "Geographic Distribution, *Gerrhonotus liocephalus infernalis*." *Herp. Rev.* 9(2):61–62.

Selcer, K. W. 1986. "Relationship Between Clutch Development and Variation in Fatbody Mass and Liver Mass of Female Keeled Earless Lizards, *Holbrookia propinqua* (Sauria: Iguanidae)." *Southwest. Nat.* 31(1):9–14.

———. 1987. "Seasonal Variation in Fatbody and Liver Mass of the Introduced Mediterranean Gecko, *Hemidactylus turcicus*, in Texas." *J. Herp.* 21(1):74–78.

Selcer, K. W., and F. W. Judd. 1982. "Variation in the Reproductive Ecology of *Holbrookia propinqua* (Sauria: Iguanidae)." *Texas J. Sci.* 34(2):125–135.

Self, J. T. 1938. "Note on the Food Habits of *Chelydra serpentina*." *Copeia* 1938(4):200.

Sherbrooke, W. C. 1981. *Horned Lizards: Unique Reptiles of Western North America*. Arizona: Southwest Parks and Monument Assoc.

Simon, C. A. 1983. "A Review of Lizard Chemoreception." Pp. 119–133 in *Lizard Ecology: Studies of a Model Organism,* edited by R. B. Huey, E. R. Pianka, and T. W. Schoener. Massachusetts: Harvard University Press.

Sites, J. W., Jr., and J. R. Dixon. 1982. "Geographic Variation in *Sceloporus variabilis,* and Its Relationship to *S. teapensis* (Sauria: Iguanidae)." *Copeia* 1982(1):14–27.

Skorepa, A. C., and J. E. Ozment. 1968. "Habitat, Habits, and Variations of *Kinosternon subrubrum* in Southern Illinois." *Trans. Illinois State Acad. Sci.* 61:247–251.

Smith, D. D. 1983. "Life History Notes, *Crotaphytus collaris* (Collared Lizard)." Reproduction. *Herp. Rev.* 14(2):46.

Smith, E. N., S. L. Robertson, and S. R. Adams. 1981. "Thermoregulation of the Spiny soft-shelled Turtle *Trionyx spinifer*." *Physiol. Zool.* 54(1):74–80.

Smith, H. M. 1933. "Descriptions of New Lizards of the Genus *Sceloporus* from Mexico and Southern United States." *Trans. Kansas Acad. Sci.* 37:263–279.

———. 1933. "On the Relationships of the Lizards *Coleonyx brevis* and *Coleonyx variegatus*." *Trans. Kansas Acad. Sci.* 36:301–314.

———. 1934. "On the Taxonomic Status of Three Species of Lizards of the Genus *Sceloporus* from Mexico and Southern United States." *Proc. Biol.*

Soc. Wash. 47:121–134.

————. 1936. "The Lizards of the Torquatus Group of the Genus *Sceloporus* Wiegmann, 1828." *Univ. Kansas Sci. Bull.* 24(21):539–693.

————. 1946. *Handbook of Lizards.* New York: Comstock Pub. Co.

————. 1946. "The Map Turtles of Texas (abstract)." *Proc. Trans. Texas Acad. Sci.* 30:60.

————. 1952. "A New Turtle from Texas." *Wasmann J. Biol.* 10(1):45–54.

Smith, H. M., and E. D. Brodie, Jr. 1982. *Reptiles of North America.* New York: Golden Press.

Smith, H. M., and S. O. Brown. 1946. "A Hitherto Neglected Integumentary Gland in the Texan Tortoise." *Trans. Texas Acad. Sci.* 30:59.

Smith, H. M., and H. K. Buechner. 1947. "The Influence of the Balcones Escarpment on the Distribution of Amphibians and Reptiles in Texas." *Bull. Chicago Acad. Sci.* 8(1):1–16.

Smith, H. M., and O. Sanders. 1952. "Distributional Data on Texan Amphibians and Reptiles." *Texas J. Sci.* 4(2):204–219.

Smith, H. M., and J. A. Slater. 1949. "The Southern Races of *Eumeces septentrionalis* (Baird)." *Trans. Kansas Acad. Sci.* 52(4):438–448.

Smith, H. M., and E. H. Taylor. 1950. "Type Localities of Mexican Reptiles and Amphibians." *Univ. Kansas Sci. Bull.* 33:319–379.

Smith, N. M. 1974. "A Taxonomic Study of the Western Collared Lizards, *Crotaphytus collaris* and *Crotaphytus insularis.*" *Brig. Young Univ. Sci. Bull.* 19(4):1–29.

Smith, P. W., and W. L. Burger. 1950. "Herpetological Results of the University of Illinois Field Expedition, Spring 1949." *Trans. Kansas Acad. Sci.* 53(2):165–175.

Sokal, R. R., and F. J. Rohlf. 1981. *Biometry: The Principles and Practices of Statistics in Biological Research.* San Francisco, California: W. H. Freeman and Co.

Stebbins, R. C. 1985. *A Field Guide to Western Reptiles and Amphibians.* Boston: Houghton Mifflin Co.

Stevenson, J. O., and L. H. Meitzen. 1946. "Behavior and Food Habits of Sennett's White-tailed Hawk in Texas." *Wilson Bull.* 58(4):198–205.

Strain, R. J. 1978. "Sexual Dimorphism as Exhibited in the Skulls of *Graptemys caglei* and *Graptemys versa.*" Honor's thesis, West Texas State University.

Strecker, J. K. 1915. "Reptiles and Amphibians of Texas." *Baylor Bull.* 18(4):1–82.

————. 1922. "An Annotated Catalogue of the Amphibians and Reptiles of Bexar County, Texas." *Bull. Sci. Soc. San Antonio.* No. 4.

————. 1927. "Observations on the Food Habits of Texas Amphibians and Reptiles." *Copeia* 1927(1):6–9.

————. 1908. "Notes on the Breeding Habits of *Phrynosoma cornutum* and Other Texas Lizards." *Proc. Biol. Soc. Wash.* 21:165–170.

————. 1926. "A List of Reptiles and Amphibians Collected by Louis Garni in the Vicinity of Boerne, Texas." *Contr. Baylor Univ. Mus.* 6:3–9.

————. 1929. "Doubtful Texas Reptile Records." Pp. 3–5 in "Random Notes on the Zoology of Texas," *Contr. Baylor Univ. Mus.* No. 18.

————. 1929. "The Eggs of *Gopherus berlandieri* Agassiz." P. 6 in "Random Notes on the Zoology of Texas," *Contr. Baylor Univ. Mus.* No. 18.

————. 1933. "Collecting at Helotes, Bexar County, Texas." *Copeia* 1933(2):77–79.

————. 1935. "A List of Hitherto Unpublished Localities for Texas Amphibians and Reptiles." *Baylor Univ. Bull.* 38(3):35–38.

————. 1935. "The Reptiles of West Frio Canyon, Real County, Texas." *Baylor Univ. Bull.* 38(3):32.

————. 1927. "Notes on a Specimen of *Gopherus berlandieri* (Agassiz)." *Copeia* 1927(3):189–190.

Strecker, J. K, and J. E. Johnson, Jr. 1935. "Notes on the Herpetology of Wilson County, Texas." *Baylor Univ. Bull.* 38(3):17–23.

Strecker, J. K., and W. J. Williams. 1927. "Herpetological Records from the Vicinity of San Marcos, Texas, with Distributional Data on the Amphibians and Reptiles of the Edwards Plateau Region and Central Texas." *Contr. Baylor Univ. Mus.* No. 12:1–16.

Sutton, G. M. 1922. "Notes on the Road-runner at Fort Worth, Texas." *Wilson Bull.* 34(1):1–20.

Tabor, S. P. 1986. "Geographic Distribution, *Terrapene ornata ornata*." *Herp. Rev.* 17(1):27–28.

Tabor, S. P., and C. T. McAllister. 1986. "Geographic Distribution, *Pseudemys scripta elegans*." *Herp. Rev.* 17(1):27.

Tanner, W. W. 1971. "A Taxonomic Study of *Crotaphytus collaris* Between the Rio Grande and Colorado Rivers." *Brig. Young Univ. Sci. Bull.* 13(2):1–29.

Tanzer, E. C., E. O. Morrison, and C. Hoffpauir. 1966. "New Locality Records for Amphibians and Reptiles in Texas." *Southwest. Nat.* 11(1): 131–132.

Telford, S. R., Jr. 1978. "Saurian Malaria in Texas." *J. Parasitol.* 64(3): 553–554.

Thomas, R. A. 1976. "A Checklist of Texas Amphibians and Reptiles." *Texas Parks and Wildlife Dept. Tech. Series* No. 17:1–16.

Thomasson, J. R. 1980. "Ornate Box Turtle, *Terrapene ornata* (Testudinae), Feeding on Pincushion Cactus, *Coryphantha vivipara* (Cactaceae)." *Southwest Nat.* 25(3):438.

Tinkle, D. W., 1961. "Geographic Variation in Reproduction, Size, Sex Ratio and Maturity of *Sternothaerus odoratus* (Testudinata: Chelydridae)."

Ecology 42(1):68–76.

Tinkle, D. W., and R. E. Ballinger. 1972. *"Sceloporus undulatus:* A Study of the Intraspecific Comparative Demography of a Lizard." *Ecology* 53 (4):570–584.

Tinkle, D. W. and D. W. Woodward. 1967. "Relative Movements of Lizards in Natural Populations as Determined from Recapture Radii." *Ecology* 48(1):166–168.

Trauth, S. E. 1978. "Ovarian Cycle of *Crotaphytus collaris* (Reptilia, Lacertilia, Iguanidae) from Arkansas with Emphasis on Corpora Albicantia, Follicular Atresia andd Reproductive Potential." *J. Herp.* 12(4):461–470.

———. 1980. "Geographic Variation and Systematics of the Lizard *Cnemidophorus sexlineatus (Linnaeus)."* 212 pp. Ph.D. dissertation. Auburn University, Auburn, Alabama.

———. 1983. "Life History Notes, *Cnemidophorus gularis* (Texas Spotted Whiptail). Hibernation." *Herp. Rev.* 14(3):73.

———. 1983. "Nesting Habitat and Reproductive Characteristics of the Lizard *Cnemidophorus sexlineatus* (Lacertilia: Teiidae)." *Amer. Midl. Nat.* 109(2):289–299.

———. 1984. "Seasonal Incidence and Reproduction in the Western Slender Glass Lizard, *Ophisaurus attenuatus attenuatus* (Reptilia, Anguidae), in Arkansas." *Southwest. Nat.* 29(3):271–275.

———. 1985. "Nest, Eggs and Hatchlings of the Mediterranean Gecko, *Hemidactylus turcicus* (Sauria:Gekkonidae), from Texas." *Southwest. Nat.* 30(2):309–310.

———. 1987. "Natural Nests and Egg Clutches of the Texas Spotted Whiptail, *Cnemidophorus gularis gularis* (Sauria: Teiidae), from Northcentral Texas." *Southwest. Nat.* 32(2):279–281.

Treadwell, R. W. 1962. "Extension of Range of Mediterranean Gecko." *Copeia* 1962(2):434–435.

Tremor, J. W. 1962. "The Critical Thermal Maximum of the Iguanid Lizard *Urosaurus ornatus."* *Diss. Abstr.* 1962, p. 1462.

Turcotte, R. 1968. "The Alligator Lizards." *Herpetology* 2(2):7.

Turner, F. B. 1977. "The Dynamics of Populations of Squamates, Crocodilians and Rhynchocephalians." Pp. 157–264 (vol. 7: Ecology and Behaviour A) in *Biology of the Reptilia,* edited by C. Gans and D. W. Tinkle. New York: Academic Press.

Turner, F. B., R. I. Jennrich, and J. D. Weintraub. 1969. "Home Ranges and Body Size of Lizards." *Ecology* 50(6):1076–1081.

Vance, T. 1978. "A Field Key to the Whiptail Lizards (Genus *Cnemidophorus*) Part I: The Whiptails of the United States." *Bull. Maryland Herp. Soc.* 14(1):1–9.

————. 1980. "Notes Concerning Locality Data on Some Texas Reptiles. Part I: New County Records." *Bull. Chicago Herp. Soc.* 15(3):70–76.

————. 1981. "Geographic Distribution, *Anolis carolinensis carolinensis.*" *Herp. Rev.* 12(1):13.

————. 1981. "*A Tentative Literary Review of Anolis carolinensis:* Taxonomic, Descriptive, Distributional and Fossil Record Literature." Corsicana, Texas: Navarro College.

————. 1983. "A Brief Survey of the Literature Concerning Sound Production of *Anolis* Lizards with Notes on *Anolis carolinensis* Voigt." *Trans. Dallas Herp. Soc.* 1983(3):1–4.

————. 1984. "A Note on the Vocalizing Ability of the Texas Spotted Whiptail Lizard (*Cnemidophorus gularis gularis*)." *Vipera* 1(7):7–9.

Veni, G. 1988. *The Caves of Bexar County.* 2nd ed. Texas Memorial Museum Speleological Monographs, 2. Univ. Texas at Austin.

Vermersch, T. G., and R. E. Kuntz. 1986. *Snakes of South-Central Texas.* Austin, Texas: Eakin Press.

Vinegar, M. B. 1975. "Life History Phenomena in Two Populations of the Lizard *Sceloporus undulatus* in Southwestern New Mexico." *Amer. Midl. Nat.* 93:388–402.

Vogt, R. C. 1982. "Genetic Sex Determination in the Spiny Softshell *Trionyx spiniferus* (Testudines: Trionychidae)." *Copeia* 1982(3):699–700.

Vogt, R. C., and S. G. Guzman. 1988. "Food Partitioning in a Neotropical Freshwater Turtle Community." *Copeia* 1988(1):37–47.

Vogt, R. C., and C. J. McCoy. 1980. "Status of the Emydine turtle Genera *Chrysemys* and *Pseudemys.*" *Ann. Carnegie Mus.* 49(5):93–102.

Voigt, W. G., and C. R. Johnson. 1976. "Aestivation and Thermoregulation in the Texas Tortoise, *Gopherus berlandieri.*" *Comp. Biochem. Physiol.* 53A:41–44.

————. 1977. "Physiological Control of Heat Exchange Rates in the Texas Tortoise, *Gopherus berlandieri.*" *Comp. Biochem. Physiol.* 56A:495–498.

Ward, J. K., A. C. Echternacht, and G. F. McCracken. 1983. "Genetic Variation and Similarity in *Anolis carolinensis* (Sauria: Iguanidae)." *Copeia* 1983(2):523–529.

Walker, J. M. 1980. "Accessory Femoral Pores in a Colony of the Collared Lizard, *Crotaphytus collaris,* in Texas." *J. Herp.* 14(4):417–418.

Walker, J. M., M. A. Paulissen, and J. M Britton. 1986. "Habitat Diversity in the Whiptail Lizard *Cnemidophorus gularis gularis* (Teiidae) in Southern Oklahoma." *Southwest. Nat.* 31(3):405–408.

Walker, J. M., S. E. Trauth, J. E. Cordes, and J. M. Britton. 1986. "Geographic Distribution, *Cnemidophorus laredoensis.*" *Herp. Rev.* 17(1):26–27.

Ward, J. P. 1984. "Relationships of Chrysemyd Turtles of North America

(Testudines: Emydidae)." *Spec. Publ. Mus. Texas Tech. Univ.* 21:1–50.

Ward, R. 1982. "Geographic Distribution, *Ophisaurus attenuatus.*" *Herp. Rev.* 13(3):80–81.

Watson, J. T. 1977. "Effects of Hypophysectomy in the Lizard *Holbrookia propinqua.*" *Texas J. Sci.* 29(3–4):255–262.

Wauer, R. 1980. *Naturalist's Big Bend: An Introduction to the Trees and Shrubs, Wildflowers, Cacti, Mammals, Birds, Reptiles and Amphibians, Fish, and Insects.* College Station: Texas A&M University Press.

Weaver, W. G., Jr. 1970. "Courtship and Combat Behavior in *Gopherus berlandieri.*" *Bull. Florida State Mus.* 15(1):1–43.

Weaver, W. G., Jr., and F. L. Rose. 1967. "Systematics, Fossil History, and Evolution of the Genus *Chrysemys.*" *Tulane Stud. Zool.* 14(2):63–73.

Webb, R. G. 1956. "Size at Sexual Maturity in the Male Softshell Turtle, *Trionyx ferox emoryi.*" *Copeia* 1956(2):121–122.

———. 1975. *Reptiles of Oklahoma.* Norman, Oklahoma: University of Oklahoma Press.

———. 1988. "Type and Type Locality of *Sceloporus poinsettii* Baird and Girard (Sauria: Iguanidae)." *Texas J. Sci.* 40(4):407–415.

Webb, W. L. 1950. "Biogeographic Regions of Texas and Oklahoma." *Ecology* 31(3):426–433.

Weniger, D. 1984. *The Explorers' Texas — The Lands and Waters.* Austin, Texas: Eakin Press.

White, J. B., and G. G. Murphy. 1973. "The Reproductive Cycle and Sexual Dimorphism of the Common Snapping Turtle, *Chelydra serpentina serpentina.*" *Herpetologica* 29(3):240–246.

Whitworth, R. J., and J. K. Wangberg. 1985. "Parasitization of the Texas Spotted Whiptail Lizard (*Cnemidophorus gularis*) by a Sarcophagid Fly (*Blaesoxipha plintopyga*): A New Host Record." *Southwest. Nat.* 30(1):163–164.

Wilbern, S. E., and D. A. Ingold. 1983. "Sexual Dimorphism in *Terrapene* shells." *Bull. Chicago Herp. Soc.* 18(2):34–36.

Wilkins, K. T., and D. J. Schmidly. 1980. "Highway Mortality of Vertebrates in Southeastern Texas." *Texas J. Sci.* 32(4):343–350.

Williams, E. E. 1983. "Ecomorphs, Faunas, Island Size, and Diverse End Points in Island Radiations of *Anolis.*" Pp. 326–370 in *Lizard Ecology: Studies of a Model Organism,* edited by R. B. Huey, E. R. Pianka, and T. W. Schoener. Cambridge, Massachusetts: Harvard University Press.

Winton, W. M. 1916. "Habits and Behavior of the Texas Horned Lizard, *Phrynosoma cornutum,* Harlan, I." *Copeia* 1916(36):81–84.

———. 1917. "Habits and Behavior of the Texas Horned Lizard, *Phrynosoma cornutum,* Harlan, II." *Copeia* 1917(39):7–8.

Wood, R. C. 1977. "Evolution of the Emydine Turtles *Graptemys* and *Mala-*

167

clemys (Reptilia, Testudines, Emydidae)." *J. Herp.* 11(4):415–421.

Worthington, R. D., and M. D. Sabath. 1966. "Winter Aggregations of the Lizard *Urosaurus ornatus ornatus* (Baird and Girard) in Texas." *Herpetologica* 22(2):94–96.

Wright, J. W. 1963. "*Cnemidophorus gularis* in New Mexico." *Southwest. Nat.* 8(1):56.

———. 1968. "Variation in Three Sympatric Sibling Species of Whiptail Lizards, Genus *Cnemidophorus*." *J. Herp.* 1(1–4):1–20.

Zucker, N. 1987. "Behavior and Movement Patterns of the Tree Lizard *Urosaurus ornatus* (Sauria: Iguanidae) in Semi-natural Enclosures." *Southwest Nat.* 32(3):321–333.

Zweifel, R. G. 1958. "The Lizard *Eumeces tetragrammus* in Coahuila, Mexico." *Herpetologica* 14:175.

Index